D0403531

ROOT CAUSE ANALYSIS
A TOOL FOR TOTAL
QUALITY MANAGEMENT

ALSO AVAILABLE FROM QUALITY PRESS

TQM: A Step-by-Step Guide to Implementation
Charles N. Weaver, Ph.D.

A TQM Approach to Achieving Manufacturing Excellence
A. Richard Shores

An Approach to Quality Improvement That Works, Second Edition
A. Donald Stratton

Management Excellence Through Quality
Thomas J. Barry

Total Quality Management: Performance and Cost Measures
Dorsey J. Talley

Baldrige Award Winning Quality
Mark Graham Brown

Leadership, Perspective, and Restructuring for Total Quality
Richard J. Pierce, editor

Quality: The Myth and the Magic
Cynthia Lane Westland

The Quality Master Plan
J. P. Russell

A Leader's Journey to Quality
Dana Cound

To request a complimentary catalog of publications,
call 800-248-1946.

ROOT CAUSE ANALYSIS

A TOOL FOR TOTAL
QUALITY MANAGEMENT

Paul F. Wilson
Larry D. Dell
and
Gaylord F. Anderson

ASQC Quality Press
Milwaukee, Wisconsin

ROOT CAUSE ANALYSIS: A TOOL FOR TOTAL QUALITY MANAGEMENT

Paul F. Wilson, Larry D. Dell, and Gaylord F. Anderson

Library of Congress Cataloging-in-Publication Data
Wilson, Paul F.
    Root cause analysis: a tool for total quality management / Paul F. Wilson, Larry
D. Dell, and Gaylord F. Anderson
        p.   cm.
    Includes bibliographical references and index.
    ISBN 0-87389-163-5
    1. Total quality managment. 2. Problem solving. I. Dell, Larry D. II. Ander-
son, Gaylord F. III. Title.
HD62.15.W55 1993
658.5 62–dc20   92-20670
                                                    CIP

10987654

ISBN 0-87389-163-5

Acquisitions Editor: Jeanine L. Lau
Production Editor: Mary Beth Nilles
Marketing Administrator: Susan Westergard
Set in Palatino and Souvenir by Montgomery Media, Inc.
Cover design by Montgomery Media, Inc.
Printed and bound by BookCrafters.

For a free copy of the ASQC Quality Press Publications Catalog, including ASQC
membership information, call 800-248-1946.

Printed in the United States of America

 Printed on recycled paper

ASQC
Quality Press
611 East Wisconsin Avenue
Milwaukee, Wisconsin 53202

CONTENTS

10 EVENTS AND CAUSAL FACTORS ANALYSIS

11 TREE DIAGRAMS

12 OTHER STRUCTURED ROOT CAUSE ANALYSIS TECHNIQUES

13 SUMMARY

PREFACE

The purpose of this book is twofold: 1) to provide individuals and organizations with a necessary tool to reach and maintain excellence and 2) to effect continual improvement. This book explores the *real* reasons for current organizational problems. It describes this concept of real or root causes as well as the analytical methods that can be used to identify them objectively. The authors further demonstrate the use of effective root cause analyses as one of the necessary steps in developing and implementing a viable productivity and quality improvement program, such as total quality management.

The book could be subtitled *Effective Problem Solving*, because the methodology could be applied in generic fashion to almost any problem. Another subtitle might be *Working Smarter, Not Harder* because the obvious idea of fixing problems to prevent their recurrence also is presented.

The primary emphasis, however, is on identifying the most obvious opportunities for improvement in present operations; in fact, on preventing problems or faults from being introduced into the system in the first place.

The book emphasizes that the discovery, rectification, and prevention of problems is everyone's responsibility. It seems obvious that any productivity and quality improvement program, to be truly effective, must develop and maintain the interest, awareness, and participation of all members of any organization. This text should therefore be of considerable interest not only to analysts, but managers, supervisors, and other individuals in any organization.

The techniques are broadly described to ensure successful application in almost any situation. The authors have included a variety of examples to demonstrate the use of root cause analyses. For those who wish to sharpen their analytical skills, there is a companion workbook available. This workbook contains more detailed case studies with work-along solutions as further illustration of concepts provided in this book.

In summary, then, this book provides practical advice on one of the more vital aspects of a total quality management program: identification of the real obstacles to organizational improvement.

ACKNOWLEDGMENTS

In compiling a book of this breadth, it becomes almost impossible to acknowledge all those individuals who have made significant contributions to this collective body of knowledge. A partial listing of these contributors is in the Suggested Reading list at the back of this book.

This text's origins are in courses developed for the Quality Resource and Training Center (QTRC) in Richland, Washington. The QTRC is a unique collaboration of contractors at the Hanford site, which is owned and managed by the Department of Energy (DOE). One of the driving forces behind this effort continues to be R. Pierre Saget, the current DOE director of the Office of Performance Assessment.

In addition, this book contains practical insights and suggestions obtained from the large number of participants in previous courses, as well as from some of the other QTRC root cause analysis instructors, including Don Kidder from the Washington Public Power Supply System and Chris Bosted, chief of the Quality Assessment Branch, Department of Energy, Richland Field Office.

No list of acknowledgments would be complete without recognizing the indulgence and moral support provided by the authors' wives: Anne, Irish, and Teresa, as well as their children, who became de facto widows and orphans during this book's lengthy preparation. Paul F. Wilson, Jr., also provided material assistance by preparing "father figures," the computer artwork used for most of the illustrations contained in this text.

1

ROOT CAUSE ANALYSIS AN INTRODUCTION

"Whatever is worth doing at all, is worth doing well."
—Philip Dormer Stanhope, Earl of Chesterfield,
Letters, March 10, 1746

Introduction

Over the years a number of improvement programs have been introduced, whose primary aim was to either reduce the number of defects produced or to emphasize the value of defect-free processes or performance. These programs include: zero defects, quality circles, PRIDE (Professional Results in Daily Efforts), and, most recently, total quality management (TQM). The basic theme of all these programs is remarkably similar: Do it right the first time.

Those individuals who have been involved in the implementation of any of these programs realize that their success or failure was directly related to a number of elements. These include:

- The real (vs. perceived) organizational commitment
- The careful analysis of current operations and/or processes

- The willingness to make any needed changes and to install necessary controls
- The taking of appropriate corrective, adaptive, and preventive actions to preclude recurrence of unwanted conditions

Although issuing policy statements, devising slogans, putting up posters, writing commitment messages, conducting rallies or meetings, and other similar activities are helpful, they will not (by themselves) make these programs work. These activities are principally to indicate intention, provide the framework for plans, set broad guidelines, and stimulate interest. If nothing further is done, it is frustrating, if not detrimental in the long run, to continue to exhort people to *improve* without defining the expectations. Specific, tangible goals must be set and focus provided to these general concepts for a viable, definitive program to eventually emerge. It is imperative that the organization firmly commit to a well-defined and long-term improvement mission. This mission will require that an ownership attitude be adopted by all participants and perhaps eventually foster a complete culture change. Successful implementation also will require that the program be installed on a firm foundation. Unfortunately, most of the current TQM literature does not mention these front-end requirements. Without these requirements being acknowledged, however, management has essentially been sold a car without an engine, or given the task of building a structure without tools or blueprints.

There are no shortcuts. Improvement or melioration implies making better, more useful or valuable, or increasing or advancing in worth or excellence. To move in any direction purposely, it is easiest to start in the right direction. Two reference points are needed to plot this direction: the destination and the origin. At the very least, the navigator must know current position and intended direction, even if the final destination is unclear.

Quality and productivity improvement, often described as a journey, must also be planned using current process/operation knowledge as a starting point (the present position) along with either the destination (goal) or intended direction (strategies) provided. Realistic improvement plans must factor in the understood limitations of the current process. If targeted performance exceeds these present limitations, then the improvement plans must address those basic changes that must be made to the activity, operation, or process in order to reach the targeted performance. All of this suggests that process capability and similar analyses should be conducted and the results used in planning or designing improvements; it is unrealistic to set improvement targets that cannot be obtained. Streamlining, automation, and other improvements will not produce the desired results if the reasons for defects and errors are not first identified and evaluated.

Once needed improvements or changes are introduced to meet the target objectives, then appropriate quantitative and/or qualitative feedback measures must also be installed to ensure that these objectives are met and maintained.

For example, one of the familiar tools of quality control that might be contemplated is statistical process control (SPC). However, the larger issues involved in TQM suggest that SPC be included in the broader category termed effective project/process management. This category also encompasses concepts of systematic analysis of processes and activities to ensure the least variation in product, performance and processes, validation concepts, and a number of related techniques.

Recent surveys of quality assurance practitioners and managers confirm that the concept of total quality ranked first; however, most of these same surveys reveal that many of the tools or elements required to successfully implement an effective total quality program also ranked high (quality planning, process capability analysis, statistical control charts, etc.). This suggests that most practitioners and managers recognize this vital linkage of the program concept with the basic techniques needed to make it work.

In addition to the techniques listed above, root cause analysis can be a powerful tool to help determine current obstacles to improvement, as well as identify those particular areas in which operation/process improvements might produce the greatest benefit. This presumes that an organizational environment or corporate culture has been established in which people are not afraid to report problems, and management recognizes their potential as an opportunity (or mandate) for improvement. This favorable climate also assumes that an effective problem reporting system has been put in place, one that accurately identifies and categorizes faults in the system.

Given that suitable mechanisms have been implemented for the collection and evaluation of real or potential problems, then the reason they manifest themselves can be carefully evaluated. As the name implies, the *root* cause is that most basic reason a problem has (or could) occur. The term "root cause analysis" encompasses a variety of techniques, both informal and structured, that may be used to determine these causes. Root cause analysis techniques are most often used in the reactive mode, i.e., to uncover the reason for problems that have already occurred. Root causes of these problems must be clearly identified and properly corrected if any real improvement is to be expected. The root causes of current problems should also be considered when planning any changes, since they may re-infect the new system. Throughout this book, these same root cause analysis techniques will be recommended for use in a proactive or forward-looking sense to analyze activities or processes with the purpose of preventing future problems from occurring.

The use of these root cause analysis techniques on a continual, day-to-day basis (rather than being used only when there is a problem) makes sense. Most of the techniques described in this book are effective problem-solving tools. An important measure of the effectiveness of problem solving is that problems are solved in a manner so that they do not recur or spread. The attitude in the organization should be that problems are everyone's responsibility, even if they appear to occur in only one area. Apparently trivial problems can sometimes affect the overall operation and result in inefficiencies or potential customer dissatisfaction. Trivial problems can combine or grow to become major problems. Another aspect of effective problem solving is that problems are correctly tagged. Production problems, for example, might be traced to design oversights or the failure to allow for manufacturing or material variations. The design itself might be modified to reduce or eliminate the problem. Teamwork and sharing of responsibility are, therefore, essential to any real progress toward problem elimination and the improvement of overall quality and productivity.

Effective problem solving is definitely a higher level skill, encompassing knowledge, ability, and experience. It involves more than the application of tools or techniques, in which training and practice will normally provide some degree of competency. Previous quality, management, and technical training provided personnel understanding of techniques such as statistical process control (SPC), trend analysis, process capability studies, Pareto analysis, and others. There is little integration of these techniques into effective problem-solving training. Numerous surveys indicate, however, that the top-ranked employee skill is problem-solving. The skills for supervisory and management personnel generally rank problem-solving after communicating management commitment, defining customer requirements, and other perceived supervisor/manager skills. These interesting results reinforce a TQM concept (in fact, one carried forward from traditional management concepts) that problems should be solved at the lowest possible organizational level.

Perspective
It has been observed that those who fail to learn from the lessons of history are condemned to relive them. Insight gained from previous mistakes or oversights can be gainfully employed in preventing their repeti-

tion. Learning from mistakes is a hard way to learn, but continuing to make the same mistakes is far harder and certainly more costly. In a competitive environment, embedded inefficiencies may be the ultimate failure-producing mechanism; in certain situations, mistakes can be disastrous. Numerous examples can be provided of industries struggling (and some failing) as a result of the added burden of repeated errors. One of the best indicators of wasted effort is rework or repair. Often, personnel and managers seem to routinely accept these inefficiencies or unwanted conditions. Somebody has to pay the bill and customers or clients are becoming increasingly unwilling to foot these costs. These cost burdens, along with resulting schedule delays, losses in productivity, or increased litigation, are adversely impacting the competitiveness of many firms.

In certain industries, the cost of mistakes cannot be calculated as easily. The nuclear power generation industry is an excellent example. The Nuclear Regulatory Commission recently focused on licensee corrective action programs. Particular attention has been given to the effectiveness of preventing recurrence of identified problems. The nuclear power industry, perhaps more so than others, also deals with problems that are only postulated as well as those that have already occurred.

Whether for reasons of competitiveness or to reduce potential liabilities, improved performance becomes an imperative. While defect-free performance is theoretically possible, it can only be accomplished with constant diligence. If absolute perfection is difficult to achieve, much less maintain, then continual improvement becomes the logical alternative. Organizations that have achieved some success in these areas, however, cannot simply rest on their laurels; disaster can be waiting around the next corner. There also is the added uncertainty of whether the improved (and apparently satisfactory) operations actually are good enough. The question is interesting because most people have some vague idea of what "good enough" means. People might feel, for example, that if they're doing the right thing 99.9 percent of the time, that's good enough. That may be adequate in any number of situations, but in others the effects caused by that 0.1 percent may be unacceptable. The following list shows what doing it right 99.9 percent of the time might lead to in the United States today:

- One hour of unsafe drinking water per month
- Two unsafe landings at O'Hare Airport every day
- 16,000 lost pieces of mail per hour
- 20,000 incorrect drug prescriptions each year
- 500 incorrect surgical operations performed each week
- 50 newborn babies dropped at birth by doctors each day
- 22,000 checks deducted from the wrong account each hour

- No telephone service or television transmission for nearly 10 minutes each week
- Your heart fails to beat 32,000 times each year

The above listing dramatically demonstrates that a quality index of 99.9 percent may not always be good enough. This could introduce the rather melancholy idea that very few things are good enough. Instead of travelling this dark path, it is perhaps better to consider a twist on the bumper sticker distributed by teachers, which states: "If you think education is expensive, consider the cost of ignorance." Our modified sticker would state: "If you think the effort involved in improvement is not worth it, consider the cost of failure."

Continued improvement inexorably will cause the overall focus and competence of the organization to shift. This shift is from problem solving to problem preventing, which will result in the best possible quality and productivity, and therefore the lowest manufacturing or service cost. Once successfully launched on its continual improvement journey, the organization will begin to uncover and correct current operational, service, or product faults. The immediate result is that these faults will be corrected and not continue downstream to the user. As the effort progresses, many of these problems will either be totally eliminated or detected far enough in advance to prevent their becoming major problems. As the organization further develops its skills most, if not all, potential problems will be eliminated from the system by careful product or operations readiness planning. Most of today's companies are struggling with the problem-solving stage, but many firms have moved into the higher-level competencies described above.

There is a cost to not moving forward. To gauge the cost of problems that are swept downstream to the customer, consider that

- For every "wronged" customer who complains, 26 others remain silent
- 91 percent of dissatisfied customers will never purchase goods or services from you again
- The average "wronged" customer will tell 8 to 16 others
- It costs about five times as much to attract new customers as it costs to keep old ones

Although the above may vary somewhat depending on the particular situation, it remains a fact that living with, rather than eliminating, problems can be costly.

Of course, in the best of all possible worlds, problems simply do not occur. Unfortunately, in real life, they do. Solving them as they occur should allow you to at least keep up; more often than not, however, the same problem is continually re-solved. The particular symptom might have been treated, but the problem's real cause was not. So, even if the number of problems never grew larger, the problem re-solving process might never end. Meanwhile, new problems were being added to our pile.

For the problem solving process to be effective, the evaluation must therefore uncover and correct the condition's root cause, not just treat the symptom(s). As you remember, root cause analysis is the process of getting at the root of a problem, its source. Like weeds, problems may only reappear if not properly removed or treated. Perhaps more ominously, they also can spread to other areas.

Generally speaking, we all like to settle matters once and for all. Things we know are wrong (or not quite right) annoy us. The inability to solve issues, whether simple or complex, can lead to continued frustration. Perhaps some of the problems we live with are not yet at the required frustration or anxiety level to prompt action. We simply accept them as inevitabilities. After all, it's just the system or the way things are. It would seem obvious that when serious problems occur it is to our advantage, if only to our peace of mind, to solve them in the quickest, most effective manner. Despite what seems obvious, this is not always done. This may be due to: resource problems, time constraints, failure to recognize the implications of inaction, misplaced/lack of priorities, or other reasons.

One pundit observed that management depends on a steady source of problems to justify its existence. We all recognize the stereotype of the overworked manager: putting in excessive overtime just trying to stay ahead of veritable tidal waves of paperwork, while at the same time being constantly disrupted by jangling telephones, anxious bosses, and a horde of peers and subordinates pressing for answers to their particular concerns. Unfortunately, some managers uncannily resemble this exaggerated stereotype. Organizations find themselves fighting one brush fire after another, with little time for anything else. Like a plane in a tailspin, they are locked into what will be later described as the *corrective action spiral*; the predictable outcome can be just as disastrous.

Root Cause Analysis
and Total Quality Management

Total quality management means "doing the right thing right the first time." This simple concept should be considered in planning as well as the conduct of activities and operations. Total quality efforts also can be directed at improving existing processes. Total quality management focuses on achieving customer satisfaction. One of TQM's key concepts is to continually exceed, rather than simply meet, these expectations. Top management support and commitment obviously are vital to the development and implementation of an effective TQM program. Beyond this commitment, the program also requires that certain elements are in place. In addition to root cause analysis of problems, other elements needed to implement an effective TQM program include:

- A means of defining and updating client/customer expectations and translating these into internal goals and objectives
- Utilizing, developing, and empowering human resources; treating these resources as capital and input to the system
- Identifying and effecting continual improvement in all areas
- Developing and implementing effective project and process management strategies; this includes control techniques such as statistical process control and others
- Appropriate quantitative measurement techniques, including analysis of both positive and negative trends
- Performance-based assessment of ongoing activities with feedback to planning and other management functions
- Positive fault correction, including effective corrective and preventive actions as well as proper adaptive actions

The pieces, depicted in Figure 1.1, are shown completing the TQM picture.

It could be argued that if a TQM program were totally effective, some of the elements which focus on problems are not necessary. However, if "doing the right thing right the first time" represents the ideal situation, then "doing the right thing right the second time" seems the next best thing. Root cause analysis can help identify the more obvious and needed improvements to current operations, since it focuses on present obstacles. Therefore, root cause analysis techniques can be used to identify these likely opportunities for improvement, as well as provide the road map for their attainment.

Root cause analysis is only one of the many tools that should be used to support any TQM effort. Used in a reactive mode, it can prevent problems from recurring. Used in a proactive mode, it can examine current operations and help to identify areas and activities that can be improved. Both uses of root cause analysis techniques will be discussed in this book. There are a wide range of root cause analysis techniques. Emphasis will be given to fitting the analysis effort to the relative importance of the problem (in the reactive mode) or to the magnitude of proposed changes (in the proactive mode). Another attribute of effective root cause analysis is its timeliness, which is directly related to the amount of time and effort expended during the analysis and framing of solutions. The concept of measured response will be covered in further detail in Chapter 6.

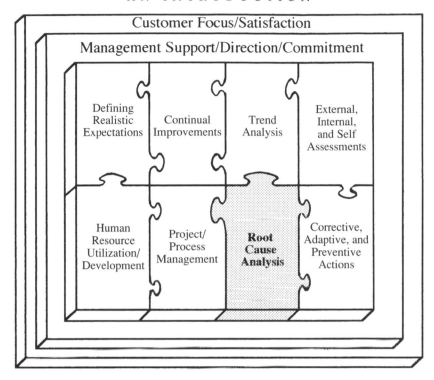

Figure 1.1
Elements of Total Quality Management

Definition

Root cause is that most basic reason for an undesirable condition or problem which, if eliminated or corrected, would have prevented it from existing or occurring. Taken in this context, the root cause is always negative. The root cause may be described in a binary sense (i.e., its existence or evidence to the contrary) or in a qualitative sense, meaning that measures intended to preclude its occurrence may be missing or less than adequate. Root causes usually are defined in terms of specific or systematic factors. Since the definition states that it is the most basic cause, a root cause usually is expressed in terms of the least common organizational, personal, or activity denominator. Root cause analysis refers to the process of identifying these causal factors, whether it be informal or structured in approach.

In keeping with the definition of root cause already given, care must be taken to distinguish symptoms clearly from causes, as well as apparent causes from root causes. Symptoms are the tangible evidence or mani-festation(s) indicating the existence or occurrence of something wrong. For example, in medicine, a symptom (e.g., fever) often accompanies and results from disease in the body. Symptoms are not the cause (the disease) but are the manifestations of the problem. A fever can be detected easily with a thermometer, but this does not identify its cause.

Similarly, root cause analysis efforts often fail due to the inability to clearly distinguish between apparent and root causes. Apparent causes represent the immediate or obvious reason for a problem. Of course, the apparent cause may turn out to be the root cause, but until this is confirmed by analysis, this assumption should not be made. All too often, causes assigned by those who are directly involved with, observe, or relate an event or occurrence are not totally reliable. This becomes clear when interviewing witnesses to an accident. Since this testimony is often clouded by emotions and confusion, it should be considered to be no more than what it is: the testimony of witnesses. Although this input may prove valuable later, it should not serve as the basis for the analysis. It should be separated into its components—only the *facts* of the event or occurrence should be used.

The importance of maintaining this distinction lies in the fact that if only the symptoms or apparent causes are treated, then the problem or fault may recur. This is depicted in Figure 1.2. The event or fault is manifested or evidenced by symptoms. Based on these symptoms, an apparent cause may be assigned. Corrective action(s) can resolve the apparent cause, but it is only when the real reason the fault or event occurred (the root cause) is identified and treated that recurrence can be prevented.

Another basic caution that needs to be provided is the relationship of the immediate cause of a problem or event and the root cause. Once again, the two should be carefully distinguished since they may not be the same. Like the apparent cause, the immediate cause is the most likely explanation for the deviation. In this case, it has been iden-tified as the trigger. The temptation often is to go no further, since here is the "smoking gun." This causal factor, however, may be derived from or otherwise simply be a manifestation of a more basic root cause.

Root cause analysis techniques are designed to provide the proper focus for identifying and resolving problems as well as potential occur-rences. This focus is designed to provide input to the management decisions regarding quality and productivity improvement on a long-term basis. Root cause analysis can be an effective management tool for finding the true or actual cause of unwanted events or conditions,

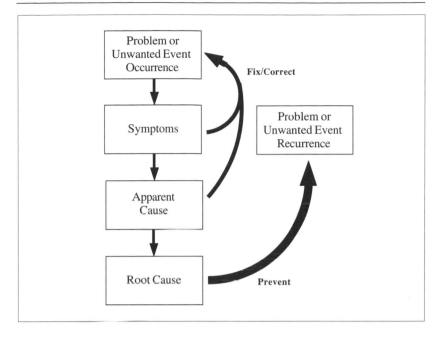

Figure 1.2
Apparent and Root Causes

facilitating effective corrective action, and preventing their recurrence. Root cause analysis can also provide the most obvious opportunities for improvement since it identifies obstacles and the basic reasons for problems in current activities or processes.

Advantages

In addition to the benefits just described, some of the specific advantages of performing effective root cause analyses include:

- Providing enhanced utilization of available resources
- Avoiding unnecessary disruptions
- Ensuring objective problem solving
- Facilitating development of a comprehensive set of solutions
- Predicting other problems
- Identifying, assembling, and integrating contributory circumstances
- Focusing on preventing recurrence, as well as providing immediate corrective action
- Identifying improvement opportunities

Each of these advantages is discussed in further detail below. These advantages, while described separately, are not exclusive of each other and tend to accrue collectively.

Enhanced Utilization of Available Resources

Effective root cause analysis provides better utilization of available resources in many ways. Personnel spend less time re-solving problems attributed to the same cause. Analyzing and remedying problems is time consuming; even a partial or inadequate solution requires that sufficient data be assembled and analyzed. Each successive re-solution of problems with the same root cause is obviously wasteful, since the effort could have been avoided if the root cause had been identified and dealt with properly the first time. Unfortunately, many organizations devote an inordinate amount of their resources to fighting fires or running in place, and therefore are unable to reach their original or defined goals. Successfully avoiding repetitive problems by attacking their root cause will improve efficiency by the simple elimination of rework. Personnel may then be utilized for other more productive and positive tasks.

Avoidance of Unnecessary Disruptions

Process flow and activity disruptions are costly, especially those due to reasons that could have been corrected. Avoidable interruptions often are the result of repeat occurrences of the same or similar problems traceable to identical basic, underlying causes. Interruptions include schedule slippages, project restarts, process or manufacturing line stoppages, outages, or system failures. These (avoidable) interruptions must be considered prohibitively expensive, since no benefit is derived from their cost. Unfortunately, many of these interruptions and continual re-corrections are routinely accepted as the norm, without anyone questioning the validity of this assumption. Unfortunately, the questions "Why are we doing this?", "Why did this happen again?" or "Can't we do better?" are not asked often enough. When maintaining the norm establishes the basis for acceptable performance, improvement seems less urgent. In fact, improvement seems necessary only when the norm finally becomes unacceptable. Acceptance of the norm has several basic embedded flaws including:

■ The conditions that result in the current norm are static.
■ The norm, if maintained, will always be satisfactory.
■ There will always be sufficient time and allowances made for any corrections when they become necessary.

In reality, we live in a world in which change is occurring at an exponential rather than linear fashion. This is easily demonstrated. Some people who travel at several hundred miles per hour, over seven miles above the Earth, coast to coast in a matter of a few hours, were alive when the Wright Brothers flew their kitelike craft the first few feet at Kitty Hawk. Within that same person's lifetime, we have landed men on the moon, routinely accept space shuttle flights, and now discuss the prospect of an Earth-orbiting, manned space station. It all is so normal now. In this age of increasing expectations, continual progress and improvement is the ultimate measure of success. Improvement becomes a continual process, a journey for which there is no ultimate destination. Eliminating current obstacles to improvement is perhaps one of the best uses of effective root cause analyses.

Objectivity in Problem Solving

Decision theory is based on choosing among alternatives using quantifiable measures. These measures may be payoffs associated with each alternative (or expected payoffs, if probabilities are assigned the likelihood of their occurrence). When subjectivity becomes a factor in the decision-making process, the analysis techniques become invalid, since it is almost otherwise impossible to predict which alternative will be chosen without detailed knowledge of personal preferences.

One of the advantages of root cause analysis, particularly the structured methods discussed in subsequent chapters, is their inherent objectivity. The analyst is guided through a well-defined, prescriptive process to reach the final conclusion. It is difficult (although not impossible) to come up with a predetermined or subjective solution. To affect this predetermined outcome, any number of conditions would have to either be modified or artificially introduced. In addition, these contrived statements would need to appear in a clearly logical fashion for the results to be considered plausible. At best, this is difficult to do.

Root cause analysis techniques also tend to prevent partial or incomplete solutions. Determining the root cause typically requires the complete event or situation to be examined. This assembly process minimizes potential omissions. Assembly and logic errors also are minimized since each piece of the process must fit the previous as well as other pieces.

Aid in Developing Solutions

Root cause analysis techniques, properly applied, will identify the true cause of the problem or event. Although the root cause analysis techniques themselves do not provide proposed solutions, the stage has been set through problem and cause definition for an effective, comprehensive set of solutions to be developed. In addition, the analysis process itself may suggest solutions. For example, in change analysis, evaluating the differences between an event and a non-event situation may point out the need for further change, evaluation of the implementation, or counter changes. If barrier analysis is employed, then re-examining the barriers that failed (or were less than adequate) might suggest further methods that are needed, improvements to current mechanisms, or other similar solutions to prevent the recurrence of the event. This (sort of reverse) examination may be conducted with most root cause analysis techniques. Sorting through the evidence and facts often suggests options that might have otherwise gone unnoticed. The development of a comprehensive set of solutions is covered in further detail in Chapter 5.

Prediction of Other Problems
Whether occurring as the logical extension of a problem or event investigation (reactive mode) or as part of a readiness review or search for improvement opportunities (proactive mode), root cause analysis results can be used to predict other problems. This can be done by taking a sideways look at other similar, related processes or operations, or by extending the results to analogous though otherwise seemingly unrelated areas or activities. For example, solutions derived for engineering or design document changes might be useful for controlling the accounting department's posting of debits and credits.

Solutions suggested by root cause analyses ideally result in the prevention of problems. If the same problem is prevented from recurring, the primary objective of performing the root cause analysis has been accomplished; however, another benefit often overlooked is the series effect that solving that particular problem might have. Often other problems, perhaps caused or exacerbated by the one that is now fixed, will disappear as well. Sometimes these fringe benefits are recognized, often they are not. Whether recognized or not, however, effective root cause analyses also can provide these unexpected but welcome results.

Assembly of Contributory Circumstances
Root cause analysis techniques, particularly the structured forms, are designed to guide the analyst through the entire analysis process. Facts, circumstances, causal factors, relationships, etc., are assembled to form the final conclusions leading to the root cause. The formality and prescription provided by the root cause analysis process prevents oversights in logic and helps identify circumstances or other events that have contributed to the event or problem under consideration. Root cause analysis techniques identify weaknesses in measures that should have otherwise prevented the event or problem from occurring in the first place, adverse effects of program or other activity changes, how one event

caused another event or had some unexpected side effects, etc. This objective collection and analysis of contributory circumstances further aids the overall understanding of processes and activities. All this information is invaluable in planning quality and productivity improvements.

Focus on Preventing Recurrence

Recurrence of events is prevented in two ways. First, since root cause analysis techniques identify problem causes at the most basic level, solutions are designed to correct the real reason they occurred or exist. Only when the taproot of the weed is removed can you reasonably expect it will not grow again. Secondly, an effective root cause analysis program usually exists only in a certain organizational climate: one dedicated to finding and solving problems with continuous improvement the prime goal. The key word is, of course, "effective"; further development of this concept is provided in Chapter 5.

Identification of Opportunities for Improvement

Root cause analysis can be used to identify the most obvious improvement opportunities by tagging current obstacles to efficient operations or activities. Existing constraints often impede progress toward overall improvement. Root cause analysis techniques originally were devised to investigate current events or problems. However, these same techniques can be readily applied in the forward (proactive) sense to look for and avoid potential program or system failures. Perhaps the fullest potential of a root cause analysis program is realized when the techniques are used in this manner.

Linkages

Root cause analysis is a management tool. Its use and fit within the usual defined management functions is discussed in detail in Chapter 2. In this section, however, we will compare the relationship and linkages of root cause analysis techniques with other current management techniques, such as those suggested by performance-based and validation concepts. Root cause analysis techniques already have been identified as one of the management tools used to construct an effective productivity and quality improvement program such as total quality management; however, root cause analysis is not the only tool needed, no more than a house can be built with a hammer alone. Other tools are required. In a program sense, these tools include process capability studies, effective status and trend reporting, development of suitable performance indicators, discipline of operations, planning, personnel training, statistical process control, etc.

Use as a Management Tool

The definition of a root cause was provided previously. Developing and implementing effective root cause techniques is considered one of the necessary tools or elements of any improvement program. The following statement summarizes this concept:

Root cause analysis can be an effective *management tool* for finding the true or actual cause of events, facilitating corrective action, and preventing their recurrence.

Although it is important to remember that the prevention and correction of problems are everyone's responsibility, not just management's, the usual inference in evaluating performance is that management is somehow *more* responsible. As in sports, the players receive the credit when the team wins, but the coach is always at fault when the team is losing. Whatever perspective is adopted, the root cause analysis results and proposed solutions ultimately will result in recommendations to management. If these recommendations are ignored or ineffectively implemented, or adequate resources are not applied, then the root cause analysis effort, however elegant, is doomed to eventual failure. Consider the mixed results achieved in implementing quality circles. The failures were almost exclusively attributed to management's disregard for suggested improvements.

Performance-Based Concepts

Root cause analysis techniques represent a return to the fundamental concepts of quality assurance: the assurance of achieved quality and the elimination of barriers preventing less-than-adequate performance. These same objectives also are the bases for the more recently introduced performance-based assessment concepts. Both root cause analysis and performance-based techniques emphasize the assurance or attainment of appropriate and satisfactory performance (as opposed to program compliance) by the direct observation and assessment of actual performance. Problems associated with implementing both concepts are remarkably similar. Both tend to factually represent or mirror actual conditions. Like a mirror they can display an unflattering image. An effective root cause analysis or performance-based assessment system may tell a story nobody wants to hear. We can either kill the bearer of bad news or listen to the truth, however painful it may be.

Both performance-based assessments and root cause analysis efforts require high-caliber personnel. Auditors who are familiar with compliance-based assessment techniques may be altogether unsuitable for performance-based assessments because they either lack the necessary perspective or do not possess a sufficient technical/operations background or needed experience to be truly effective. Many root cause analysis programs fail because the personnel assigned these duties are unable to correctly interpret data, lack training in the techniques, or do not have the needed technical/operations experience. Program, operations, or system evaluations require fairly senior personnel to be effective.

Approach Used in This Book

This book consists of two distinct, major parts. The first part (Chapters 1 through 7) contains an examination of root cause and analysis concepts, its use as a management tool, getting an effective program started, applying the results, and evaluating proposed solutions. The second part (Chapters 8 through 12) consists of detailed discussions of selected root cause analysis techniques. Each of these sections provides a description of the technique, including its advantages and disadvantages. This book's intent is to provide a reasonably balanced presentation of root cause analysis to allow first-level supervisors and managers, as well as prospective analysts, to benefit from its reading. It should be useful as a guide for anyone interested in developing more effective problem-solving methodologies.

An accompanying workbook is available for readers who wish to pursue the subject further or sharpen their analytical skills. In the workbook, more detailed case studies are provided, along with sample analyses, the development of proposed solutions, and their evaluation.

Summary

Through the years, a number of quality and productivity improvement programs have been introduced. Their success or failure has been largely influenced by a number of organizational factors, but also because the proper foundations were not set in place. A number of these elements are needed, one of which is root cause analysis. Root cause analysis can be an effective management tool for finding the true or actual cause of events, facilitating corrective action, and preventing their recurrence. Its use as a management tool is covered in Chapter 2.

2

ROOT CAUSE ANALYSIS A MANAGEMENT TOOL

"Things are not always what they seem."

—Phaedrus,

Fables, 8 A.D.

Introduction

This chapter will discuss the use of root cause analysis techniques as a management tool. To accomplish this, we will first characterize the basic functions of management, then assemble these functions and analyze them as a system or process and show root cause analysis techniques as an integral, necessary component. This approach will aid in understanding the use of root cause analysis techniques within the defined management functions of planning, organizing, directing, and controlling.

Most often, root cause analysis techniques are utilized as input to the decision-making process. When used in the reactive (problem-solving) mode, the output of root cause analyses provides objective identification of organizational faults. There usually is little interpretation required since the techniques should clearly depict things the way they are, not what they seem or appear to be. In the proactive or predictive mode, the same techniques are useful to identify and thereby avoid future mistakes.

Management routinely makes decisions relative to each of its defined functions. These functions are highly interrelated and interdependent. The results obtained by root cause analysis techniques will be discussed as valuable input to the planning process, although they also are extremely useful in identifying problems (or improvement opportunities) related to the other management functions of directing, organizing, and controlling.

Any productivity or quality improvement program requires long-term organizational commitment. Simply putting into place all the necessary components (subsystems) takes time; the process of change requires that additional time be allowed for the installed systems to take effect; required modifications or the installation of other, required subsystems also takes time. Change should be recognized as a continual process that requires constant management support and direction. The improvement process often is described as a journey to illustrate this point, one that starts once the organization decides to commit to this course. The starting point for this journey is represented by the current status. Each organization has a varying degree of readiness; this suggests one of the first orders of business will be some sort of readiness review or self assessment. Before attempting to effect productivity or quality improvement, some effort will be required to objectively determine current capabilities and to realistically assess plans and any proposed changes. How can you embark on this (or any other) journey if you have no concept of where you are now, where you want to go, or even what direction(s) you should take?

Lessons learned from faults in current operations provide prepaid and therefore valuable insight, if for no other reason than that they point out previous wrong turns or directions to avoid. We learn from our mistakes only when we have some clear idea of why they happened in the first place. Finding the *real* reasons that problems occur is the primary objective of root cause analysis. When combined with process/project management, trend analysis, human resource development, fault correction, performance-based assessments, and other tools or elements, they provide a firm foundation on which to construct an effective TQM program and almost guarantee its eventual success.

Since root cause analysis will be described as a tool, some training is required in its use. This training is not limited to technique training for designated analysts, but indoctrination and training for all personnel. This includes first-line supervisors and managers who need to be made aware of the purpose, objectives, and inherent benefit of an effective root cause analysis effort. This will develop the necessary awareness, interest, and ownership. Root cause analysis, properly implemented, will tell you the real reasons for problems. Personnel need to understand that unless the real reason(s) a problem occurs is identified and corrected, the organization will continue to have that problem and, in the long run, this is neither to the individual's nor the collective benefit.

In summary, root cause analysis can be an effective management tool for finding the true or actual cause of events, facilitating corrective action, and preventing the recurrence of problems. The results should be viewed positively as opportunities to improve current organizational efforts.

Relationship to
Normal Management Functions

Root cause analysis techniques have been described as one of the tools or elements needed to develop and implement an effective quality and productivity improvement program, such as total quality management. These techniques have further been defined as a management tool; management can be depicted as a series of specific, interrelated functions. The following discussion describes how root cause analysis techniques correlate with these functions.

The process of management has been described in enough textbooks to fill the average small town library. Most of these management texts, however, agree that this process consists of the following four major functions:

- Planning
- Organizing
- Directing
- Controlling

Although other management models may be presented, some with differing titles for these same basic functions or with a different number of functions defined, this model will suffice for our purposes. We will now demonstrate the fit of root cause analysis techniques with these four major management functions.

Planning

Root cause analysis can provide significant input to the planning function. For example, when used in the reactive or problem-solving mode, root cause analysis techniques will have identified the previous reason(s) for organizational difficulties or faults. In the process, they have helped isolate systematic or program deficiencies. Root cause analyses trace problems to their source, whether related to personnel, hardware or equipment, documentation, or other conditions. The results clearly distinguish pitfalls to avoid in the future. With objectivity, root cause analysis demarcates the historical baseline and furnishes a list of lessons learned.

While it is not argued that the same problems will necessarily occur again in the future, the information gained through the analysis process is valuable in the planning process when weighing options.

Perhaps more important than their use in effectively solving current problems, these same techniques can be used in a prospective sense to avoid potential difficulties. For example, one of the techniques discussed in Chapter 8 is change analysis. As its name implies, change analysis weighs the effects introduced by change. Another technique, barrier analysis (Chapter 9), deals with the adequacy of safeguards or barriers designed to prevent problems and unwanted events or occurrences. Both these techniques also lend themselves to postulating the effect of planned changes or considered measures. In fact, the real potential of these techniques may be in this forward-looking mode. Problem solving becomes more of a final clean-up operation for any faults which might have been overlooked and thereby avoided by careful planning.

The above has discussed the use of root cause analysis results in the planning process, one of the four management functions. It should also be pointed out that the use of these techniques might point out faults in the planning process itself. In fact, experience suggests that less-than-adequate planning is one of the more common root causes of problems.

Organizing

In organizing to perform a certain activity, it is useful to examine which areas, groups, approaches, or individuals may have worked better in the past. In TQM, this term has a broader connotation than the classical management definition of "how to organize" or "who to assign." Rather, organizing assumes the feature of *structuring* with standards of performance and effectiveness the applied measures. Previous faults identified by root cause analysis might include organizational misalignment, improper mission or function statement, missing or less than adequate resource application, inadequate operational or service coverage, etc. As previously discussed in planning, in addition to using root cause analysis techniques to provide baseline or historical information, many of these same techniques can be employed in a proactive or forward-looking mode, to help identify potential problems or difficulties in proposed organizational or task accomplishment plans. The techniques may have identified problems with the organizing aspect of the management process, helping to recognize this particular management function as the weak link between the planning and actual implementation phases of projects or activities.

Directing

Most people relate to this particular management function, assuming that it is primarily what managers do: tell others what to do. Unfortunately, this group includes many managers, who also believe this to be their most important function, with the other aspects far less critical. The resulting imbalance, particularly the neglect of planning, often results in chaos. Since the basis for requested activities is less obvious or logical, greater emphasis is placed on unquestioned authority. The eventual outcome is predictable. Even a benevolent autocracy approach ultimately will fail, since it violates one of the basic concepts of TQM, that of empowering personnel and making them responsible for their own work. Undue emphasis on this particular management function also is typified by the supervisor or manager who thinks it necessary to be intimately involved in just about everything. No detail is considered unimportant. Another perhaps more unwitting offender is the supervisor or manager who, having worked up through the ranks, still likes to keep his/her hands on "real" problems.

These stereotypes, with their singular and inappropriate focus on this management function, are prime crisis management candidates. Crisis management can be identified by any number of the following characteristics: running in place (lack of planning), confusion regarding authority and responsibility (lack of organization), and unclear expectations (lack of control). The symptoms of crisis management are readily observed: frustrated and overworked employees, missed deadlines, constantly changing objectives, and so on. Although some sympathy might be extended employees working in this environment, the real victim is the organization itself.

How can the effective use of root cause analysis techniques help? First, crisis management often is launched during the first phases of the corrective action spiral, to be described in detail later. There is an inability to get on with the business at hand caused by the constant fixing of problems, rather than solving them. Since root cause analyses reveal the real causes of these problems, correcting their cause rather than their symptoms will lead to their eventual solution. Secondly, root cause analysis may identify the specific malady itself. Root cause analysis results may clearly show that the other management activities are being overlooked or not performed adequately.

Controlling

Controlling activities, in the usual, traditional sense, involves the measurement of the results of operations or activities against plans or predetermined standards. This definition has limited meaning, however, if these predetermined expectations have not been articulated as part of an effective planning process. This leads to the broader meaning of control within TQM concepts. Control evaluates effectiveness and actual performance, in addition to compliance to established standards or measures. The emphasis is on performance, particularly to meeting client/customer expectations (whether internal or external). This introduces the interesting concept that it may be beneficial when employees are not following procedures.

Whether the wider or narrower connotation of control is subscribed to, root cause analysis results can provide the necessary feedback to the other management functions. These analysis techniques can help reduce losses, inefficiencies, and waste by using problems, events, failed practices or procedures, and similar indications of less-than-adequate conditions to pinpoint their source. The same techniques may provide valuable insight into process or activity variation by discerning assignable causes for these differences as well as clearly establishing those that should be considered random or chance (outliers). To diagnose and effectively treat any fault or difficulty, you need to know what and where the pain is before you prescribe the pill. Corrective, preventive, or adaptive action can only be judged effective when it addresses the specific situation as well as its underlying cause. It also is equally important to decide when these treatments are no longer needed. Too much control often is as bad as not having enough. Further discussion of this concept is provided in Chapters 3 and 7.

Systems Approach

System concepts are particularly useful in understanding the management process. Figure 2.1 shows a simplified feedback system. This system and its operation are described as follows. There is an input to the system, the process or activity itself with some result or output. The output is fed back (hence the name) and compared to a desired operating point. If a difference exists between the two, corrections are made to return the system to the desired operating level. Although this represents a grossly simplified accounting of the system and its operation, it is sufficient for our purpose.

The model can be applied to most situations. The operation of the system is perhaps easiest to visualize when it is applied to continuous processing activities such as manufacturing: the input is raw materials or unfinished goods, the manufacturing activity or process itself, with the resultant output of finished goods. The desired operating level for comparison purposes might be the production rate. The desired operating

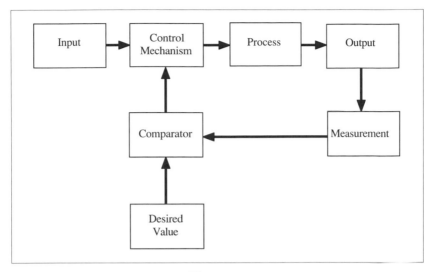

Figure 2.1
Generalized Feedback System

level could alternately be the reject rate, customer ratings, or any other attribute(s) or variable(s) for which measurement and control is proposed.

The same basic model also works well in a variety of applications, although visualization may be more difficult. For example, the system model might be employed to analyze activities within an accounting department; in this case the input might be invoices, the process, the posting of these invoices, with the output being ledger or account entries. In modeling an engineering activity, the input might be needed design changes and the output finished calculations, specifications, or drawings.

The system boundaries can be as encompassing or narrow as is necessary to help analyze the situation. Creating an analog or model of processes and activities in this fashion helps in visualizing how the overall system works. Also, to the extent that the model is a faithful replication, it allows analyzing the process or activity using some of the logic and analytical techniques developed for feedback systems. Many large companies have constructed fairly sophisticated models of their operations; this allows them to test the models by varying inputs and determining what happens without the risk of trying these innovations on the actual process or activity itself. An excellent example of the value of these analogs is the use of dummies in testing automobile and other safety equipment and devices; another would be control room or airplane cockpit simulators in training plant operators and pilots in emergency situations.

System Considerations

Feedback systems, by the corrective action process, tend to seek equilibrium or some steady-state condition. As explained previously, when differences are detected between the actual and desired condition, corrections will be made to adjust the process to eliminate these differences, ultimately bringing the process or activity to the desired operating level. However, if the corrections that can be made within the system are not sufficient to reach this point, problems will occur. Consider the simple example of the temperature in a house (Figure 2.2). The feedback system in this example is comprised of a thermostat and furnace. The temperature setting device is, of course, the thermostat. There is also a temperature sensing device within the thermostat, which opens or closes an electrical contact. The contact is closed when the temperature setting is less than the actual temperature in the house, causing the furnace to turn on. When the house temperature is raised by the furnace, the temperature sensing device causes the contact to open and the furnace turns off.

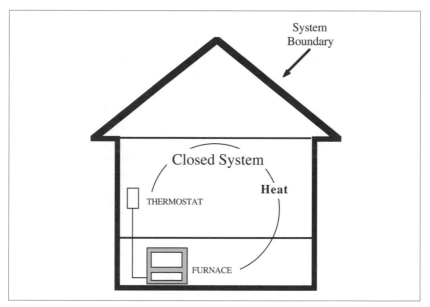

Figure 2.2
Typical Closed Loop System

The system, when initially activated, would tend to turn the furnace on until the desired temperature (setpoint) was reached and then turn off. If the closed system (the house) were in a vacuum (like a large thermos bottle), the furnace might never turn on again, since there were no external influences to cause loss of heat (Figure 2.3). However, if the outside temperature is lower than our house, the R value of our insulation is not infinity, doors are opened and closed for entry and exit purposes, heat is lost through glass windows, and so on, the temperature eventually will move down from the setpoint and the furnace will turn on again. If the furnace is improperly sized, for example—undersized in terms of supplying the needed heat output—it may stay on a long time to correct the temperature difference. This undersizing might have occurred because of less than adequate heating system design or because our closed loop system is now overwhelmed by external influences.

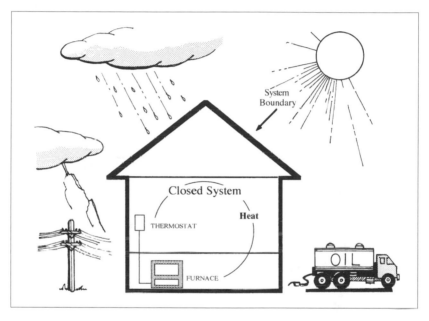

Figure 2.3
Closed System and External Forces

As an example of the latter, most heating systems are designed using historical meteorological data as a design basis. Assuming adequate design for that purpose, the system would be overwhelmed if, for example, the world was plunged suddenly into a new Ice Age. It might seem an apparent solution to install as large a furnace as possible to avert this problem, but in addition to cost-effectivity considerations and the realistic assessment of the likelihood of an unpredicted, sudden basic weather change, other system factors suggest this solution is not necessarily optimal and needs more evaluation. For example, an oversized furnace would require extremely short time periods to make the necessary temperature corrections and, in fact, most likely overshoot the setpoint before turning off due to inherent time lags in the system.

This points out another important consideration. When analyzing a system and considering alternatives, there are relatively few absolutes. Compromises are usually made that infer some risk will be assumed; it is otherwise impractical to devise a system which deals effectively with all postulated contingencies. There are, however, reasonable choices that preclude the system from being overwhelmed by unforeseen external changes, which prevent excessive overshoot, that minimize the phenomenon called *hunting* or *cycling*, and other foreseen problems. These same considerations apply to the management of a design, engineering, manufacturing, service, or any other operation or activity, as will be discussed next.

Management Analogy

The four functions of management can now be shown as a closed loop system as depicted in Figure 2.4. This model also is found in any number of management science textbooks.

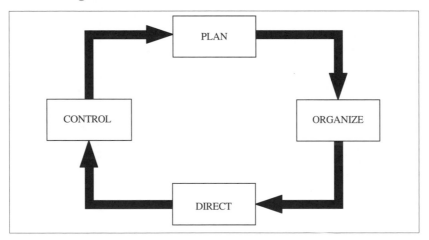

Figure 2.4
Management Analogy

The four functions of management (planning, organizing, directing, and controlling) are shown in their usual sequence, with the output from the control function feeding back to the planning process. As with other closed loop systems, the management model system also is subject to being overwhelmed by external forces, corrective action cycling, and failure to reach or maintain equilibrium (homeostasis). One particular phenomenon of interest is that of hunting or corrective action cycling. Corrective action cycling can occur when the real cause of surfaced problems is not adequately solved. In this situation, the *same* problems are continually re-solved or, more ominously, similar or related problems begin to occur. In addition, this situation could be termed the Petri dish for the crisis management virus.

Stabilizing the Management Process

Clearly, a stabilizing effect in the loop is needed to prevent corrective action cycling. This stabilization is accomplished in two steps: (1) root cause analysis to determine their real cause, and (2) providing a permanent fix. The settling down of the system is accomplished by introducing preventive (rather then strictly corrective or adaptive) measures into the loop (Figure 2.5). It will seem paradoxical to some that more effort is required to solve problems when it is difficult enough just to keep up with them, but it is the longer term perspective that is crucial.

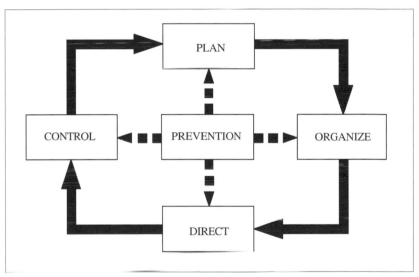

Figure 2.5
Introducing Prevention into the Loop

Clearly identifying the real causes of problems, conditions, or events is therefore the first step in stabilizing the management process. Long-term stabilization is difficult if the real problems are not being worked on. It is similar to treating the wrong disease; unless you are fortunate enough that the same treatment will also correct your particular condition, chances are fairly good you'll still have the disease.

The second step in stabilizing the system involves the application of the appropriate amount of prevention in the elimination of faults or problems. This is discussed in detail in Chapters 5 and 6.

It is unfortunate that so many organizations are overwhelmed by the problems they encounter and are expected to resolve. Practically all their time and energies are spent in a catch-up mode. As the Red Queen told Alice in *Through the Looking Glass,* "It takes all the running you can do, to keep in the same place." Running on a treadmill might seem like good exercise, but it is quite different than winning a race. What is unfortunate is that much of this wasted effort might be avoided and applied constructively elsewhere. Fixing a problem once and for all obviously requires some additional effort, but this should be viewed as an investment. Someday it will pay off; it is working smarter, not harder.

Cost Effectiveness
It also could be argued that treating faults at their root cause is, in the long run, the most cost-effective approach. Consider the costs curves shown in Figure 2.6.

The vertical axis is cost for all curves shown. The horizontal axis is the degree of preventive action(s) taken. The first curve shown is the cost of problems. If little preventive action is taken, the cost of problems continually being corrected is high. When significant preventive action(s) are taken, the cost of problems is low. However, the costs of preventive action(s)—the second curve—is just the reverse. The total cost (the third curve) is the sum of the other two, representing the cost of preventing problems and the cost of the problems themselves.

It can be seen that there is an optimum cost point. It is suggested, though not supported by empirical data, that this point corresponds to treating problems at their root cause level and using valid evaluation

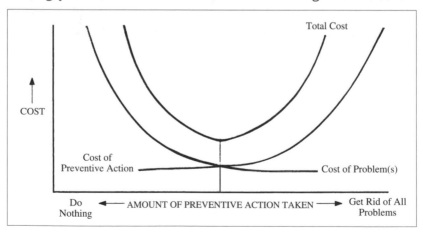

Figure 2.6
Problem, Prevention, and Total Cost Curves

techniques to determine those problems that are not worth solving. Lest the latter sound heretical, it should be added that there are situations in which preventive action is not appropriate; the entire process or activity should be overhauled. Perhaps you need to start over. If Figure 2.6 is combined with Figure 1.2, then this suggested relationship is made clearer (Figure 2.7).

Feedforward vs. Feedback Control Systems

Since we have borrowed from control theory throughout this chapter, one last topic suggests itself. So far, feedback systems have been discussed. Another control scheme, used for many processes, is the feedforward systems. Feedforward systems differ from feedback systems in that the needed correction is made as soon as a change in the input is detected. You will recall that in a feedback system, this correction was made when the change in the output was detected. This means that the response time (lag) of a feedforward system is substantially less.

However, the amount of correction needed once the change in the input is detected *must be precisely known*. Too much or too little remedy will

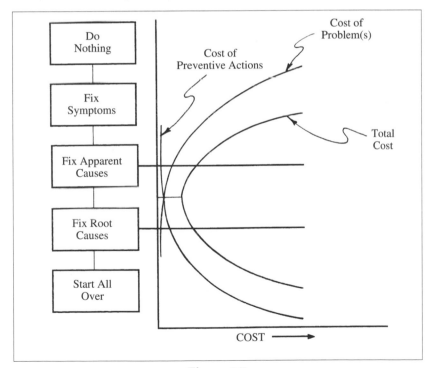

Figure 2.7
Cost Effectiveness of Treating Root Causes

not only be incorrect, but may make matters worse. Implementing a feed-forward system requires detailed knowledge of the system. For some activities or processes, this can be relatively straightforward. For others, it may require considerable study to determine the system characteristics. The advantage to applying the concept are obvious. As soon as conditions change, the proper type and amount of corrective action is applied. Fluctuations in the output of the system are thereby hopefully minimized.

In a management sense, adoption of a feedforward concept requires greater flexibility. It is probably true that few organizations are currently positioned to gain the advantage of such a system. Adopting a feedforward technique may be possible only after a substantial period of effective operation in the feedback mode. Feedforward remains an intriguing concept, perhaps something to keep in mind for the future. It's tricky to implement, but when done effectively, it provides considerable benefit. In terms of root cause analysis, it would infer the use of the techniques almost entirely in their proactive mode. There would be no problems or faults to correct, since they were detected upstream and thereby prevented from happening in the first place.

Root Cause Analysis and the Overall Management Process

Input to the Planning Process

Effective root cause analysis is a valuable input to the management planning process. It is important since it clearly identifies the real reasons for surfaced problems or unwanted conditions and events. In this context, root cause analysis provides management with a reasonably accurate profile of organizational ills. Unless these ills are treated, the chances are that these and similar problems will continue to occur. Effective planning, including the revision of current plans and policies, benefits from effective root cause analyses.

In a second sense, root cause analysis provides valuable input to the planning process by providing historical perspective. The accumulated output of an effective root cause analysis effort is perhaps the closest thing to a lessons learned primer. When applied during planning, previous problem areas may be avoided. Although there is no guarantee that the same problems will not surface again, the chance of this happening has not been changed unless the conditions which caused previous deficiencies have been eliminated.

Lastly, it will be pointed out throughout this book that root cause analysis techniques may be used in a proactive mode. Many of these techniques can be used to postulate future events and conditions. This kind of homework can be extremely valuable in avoiding potential future problems, some of which could be quite costly, thereby making it a cost-effective approach. How much effort of this type is needed? The obvious answer is that amount suggested necessary to offset the possible consequences of less-than-adequate planning. To use a simple example, the degree to which the family car is checked over prior to a short trip downtown to the store would obviously be different than that if a long vacation trip were being undertaken, even more so if most of the trip involved long-distance travel through uninhabited areas or by remote highway.

Other Management Techniques

Root cause analysis allows maximum utilization of other management techniques—for example, Pareto analysis. Pareto, an economist, noted that large amounts of wealth were concentrated among a few persons. Further developed as a management technique, Pareto analysis involves ranking problems by their significance and then concentrating on the more important. The ranking criteria may be tailored to the organization or the problem set itself. The ranking criteria generally include cost and may also include risk or probability weighting or others, such as severity or priority level assignments. Other factors might include public or worker safety, environmental considerations, legal or regulatory compliance, or potential impact on goal achievement or mission completion. Regardless of any weighting or other applied criteria, the pattern that usually emerges is one of a smaller percentage of the total number of problems being the more important. This usual pattern suggested the later interpretation of the significant few vs. the trivial many as well as the often used 80-20 rule. This implies that 20 percent of any organization's problems may cause 80 percent of their troubles.

Root cause analysis techniques obviously fit well with Pareto concepts. They help identify the real cause of problems and thereby aid in the overall classification process. In addition, the codes used in root cause analysis may be helpful in problem characterization. Some of the techniques discussed in evaluating solutions (Chapter 6) are easily adapted for Pareto analysis.

Root cause techniques also fit well with other management tools, such as trend analysis. The root cause categories (see Chapter 3) are logical groupings that may suggest criteria to measure performance. The cause categories also may be useful in conducting performance-based assessments, either as benchmarks of organizational performance or as action groupings for needed improvement(s) areas. The use of root cause analysis techniques in this manner is provided in later chapters. Results obtained from root cause analyses also are useful as input to cost or risk-benefit evaluations. The plain fact that springs from the above discussion is that a reasonably skilled and experienced practitioner can blend and merge all these management techniques into an effective program. There is, however, no universal recipe that can be followed. Organizational needs, like people's tastes and preferences, are just too complex and different to allow this.

Summary

This chapter has dealt primarily with the management aspects of root cause analysis. To understand the process of management, system concepts have been introduced to more clearly define the use of root cause analysis as a tool or element within this system. As a management tool, root cause analysis can be used with other techniques to build a firm foundation for quality and productivity programs such as total quality management.

3

GETTING STARTED

"A journey of a thousand miles must begin with a single step."

—Lao Tzu,

The Way of Lao Tzu, sixth century B.C.

Introduction

This ancient Chinese adage accurately describes this chapter's contents. We will describe the first steps involved in performing a (single) root cause analysis, as well as elements needed for an effective fault detection and root cause analysis system. Therefore, this chapter will not only discuss how to get started but also how to keep going. There are a number of these elements that eventually need to be put in place as part of an effective system, so we will describe them separately. The appropriate response to the question: "How do you eat an elephant?" is deceptively simple: "By first cutting it into bite-size pieces."

The scientific method is an accepted, systematic approach to defining and solving problems. Most individuals first encounter this technique in a high school laboratory. The first step in the scientific method is to define the problem. The second step is to formulate a hypothesis (an educated guess) regarding the problem. The third step is to gather data relevant to the problem. These first three steps will be explored in this chapter. The entire scientific method is discussed in considerably more detail in Chapter 5.

Since root cause analysis techniques most often are utilized in the reactive mode—that is, in response to identified problems or events—the first step usually is done for us. In most organizations, there is no need to search for problems on which to work. In fact, the decision to implement a root cause analysis system usually springs from a free-flowing wellhead of problems, many of them repetitive. There usually is no difficulty in deciding where to look; the only challenge might be in figuring out which one to work on first.

Defining the criteria for problem selection and selecting candidates for analysis are discussed later in this chapter. The setting up of appropriate fault detection and reporting systems, the concepts of pulse points, trend analysis, coding of problems, and other techniques for an effective ongoing problem analysis system also are covered. The real payoff for this effort comes down the road when these immediate problems have been successfully dealt with and one can begin to look for those that have not yet happened.

The ultimate objective of root cause analysis techniques (at least in the reactive mode) is to effect no further need for their use. This means that the techniques are rarely used for solving problems, because they occur infrequently, if at all. Total quality management (TQM) emphasizes continual improvement. The techniques and approaches discussed in this text could then be used in their proactive or forward-looking mode as effective tools to identify the most likely candidates for improvement and to predict and avoid any future problems.

Development and Initial Implementation

The first phases in the development and initial implementation of an effective root cause analysis program include the following:
- Setting up appropriate reporting mechanisms
- Defining criteria for problem selection
- Selecting candidates for analysis
- Selecting analysis techniques that will be utilized

Each of these will be discussed separately.

Setting Up Appropriate Reporting Mechanisms

All organizations need information on what is being done correctly, what could be done better, and what is being done incorrectly. Otherwise, the organization receives no feedback to compare operations with their desired or optimum levels, to measure progress in goal attainment, and accurately gauge customer/client satisfaction. Without this information, the organization basically is playing the familiar children's game of blindman's bluff. The only problem is that, in this version of the game, what is really at stake may be the organization's future and survival. In a competitive world, pleading nolo contendere is just the same as pleading guilty. Rarely are second chances allowed.

Organizations need to know what's going on out there. The technique of management by walking around has been strongly endorsed. In addition to its obvious aerobic value, it can provide real insight into ongoing activities and alert the managers of real or potential deficiencies in operations. It can often (but shouldn't) come as a surprise that the employees and workers know more about what's really going on than do supervisors or managers. There is no particular secret to why this occurs; the workers simply are closer to what is going on (and any problems). Ed Koch, New York City's former mayor, is an excellent example of someone who practiced this simple idea. His famous question to anyone he met was "How am I doing?" If you're willing to stop, look, and listen, there's a lot of good information out there for the taking. Or you could pay big bucks for a high-priced consultant to come in and tell you the same thing. Their usual technique is to listen to these same people.

In addition to informal feedback, organizations generally need more structured mechanisms to measure organizational performance, including fault detection and reporting. Our discussion will focus on the fault-detection system, since this ties more closely with root cause analysis needs. Depending on the particular organization or industry, this detection and reporting system would typically include system, product or service problems, unwanted events or occurrences, faulty material or processes, order returns, complaints, schedule slippages, amount of rework, etc. In short, a system which collects, assembles, and reports all those things that are undesirable, unwanted, not acceptable, or less than adequate.

This leads to the obvious questions of: How much data is required? What is appropriate? In turn these questions lead to others. Does the system detect and report all significant faults? (Significance in this sense means that the discovered faults are reliable indicators of *real* organizational problems.) Cause and effect relationships may need to be examined closely. It is easy to assume that since we have not heard about any problems in a particular area, there probably are none. Our detection level, however, may not be sensitive enough, improperly focused, or fooled. Even highly sensitive radars can be cloaked by chaff, jammed to prevent true signals, or confused by deliberate false inputs.

Given that the fault detection and reporting systems are properly focused and include all needed information, the output must also be informative, accurate, and timely. The proper people must be included in the information distribution system. Quite often, the output of a fault detection system are simply status and trend reports, which include some categorization and analysis of the information provided. However, if this categorization and analysis has been done by personnel unfamiliar with the operation or activity, considerable information value can be lost in the process. Often it can become a numbers game, with severity and importance of particular problems neglected. It should be obvious that just a few significant problems might be considerably worse than many negligible ones, although this is not suggested by the numbers alone. Each organization must decide what kinds of faults and which significance levels are collected and reported in their particular fault detection and reporting system. The system generally should:

■Provide a sufficient level of validation for organizational performance

■Identify, as a minimum, faults which could have a significant impact on the organization

■Include all aspects and activities which could be fault generators

■Provide a timely, accurate output to all affected and responsible individuals

■Serve as suitable input to other systems, such as root cause and trend analyses

As to exactly what is appropriate for any given organization, this question is easiest to answer using a *NOT* logic approach. It is easier to determine when the system is NOT working well. For example, if the organization is experiencing many unexpected problems, the routine reporting mechanisms are probably NOT adequate in providing the necessary early warnings. If clear patterns which help identify problem areas or potential systematic and program discrepancies do not emerge from the present system, it is likely NOT adequate. If client/customer dissatisfaction does not directly correlate with the number and type of faults discovered, then the system is NOT effective. This logic may seem curious, but remember that the entire idea of a fault detection and reporting system itself is based on negatives. In fact, what we are looking for is an overall absence of negatives.

This absence of negatives does not imply, however, that everything is positive. For example, an organization could be misled by the artificial silence of a gagged system. This false indication can be caused in a number of ways, such as the ineffective or biased analysis, or complete disregard of reported deficiencies. Regarding the latter, if you knew about the problem all along, chances are the reporting system worked OK. You chose not to listen; doing nothing or failing to correct or prevent the problem was your deliberate decision. It is unfortunate that often reasonably comprehensive and accurate fault detections are designed and installed, but not used. Through the intermediate processes, particularly the analysis and reporting stage, the output is unwittingly and sometimes deliberately so altered as to defeat its intended purpose.

Defining Criteria for Problem Selection

The next step, that of selecting problems for analysis, would seem relatively straightforward: simply select them in order of their importance. The difficulty arises in devising a meaningful ordering or ranking process. For example, consider what may appear to be an obvious common problem denominator: cost. Most businesses and managers can easily grasp the cost impact of a problem, which seems to be a factor that can be quickly and easily computed. However, consider a major problem which (apparently) has resulted in reduced sales. Not only are missed sales not easily quantified, but the estimate requires one make the simplifying assumption that all or some portion of these losses are attributable to this problem. There is another consideration: Which cost will be used as the eventual problem-ranking criterion? Should it be the estimated lost sales caused by the problem, the cost to fix the problem, expected cost reductions (or revenue increases) once the problem is fixed, or another value?

Some problems are difficult to quantify in terms of dollars. For example, what about employee or public safety issues? How might the costs of compliance be measured? What value should be assigned to loss of goodwill? How do you quantify lost opportunities? The list of problems encountered when assuming that cost alone is a sufficient discriminator could go on and on. The previous listed cautions are not intended to suggest that cost alone might be sufficient in ranking faults, but is only intended (as will be pointed out with other measures) that care be used in the application of any ranking criteria.

Further discussion on evaluation criteria is contained in Chapter 6. Organizations may wish to assign composite weighting factors in ranking problems. For example, cost might be assigned a weight of 0.4 or 40 percent, risk or safety priority a weight of 0.4 or 40 percent, and organizational impact a weight of 0.2 or 20 percent. The final score also could then be multiplied by the chance of recurrence or some other probability factor, resulting in an expected value. What is best for one organization may not work well with another. For example, financial institutions and others with high fiduciary trust aspects or operational risk characteristics might display a strong aversion to risk of any kind and therefore choose to make this factor 80 percent of the total weight, while others, such as high-tech venture companies, may not wish to consider the risk factor at all.

Problems also may be ranked in terms of their organizational priority, their consequence or severity, as well as their real or potential hazard. Scales and tables may be derived for this purpose. Another ranking criterion might be safety impact. Yet another might be assessed customer displeasure characteristics. The list continues.

All of the above suggest that the ranking criteria applied to problems can vary between industries and service sectors within segments of these industries, and perhaps even within individual organizations or departments within these companies. Whatever ranking criteria that will be used, however, should be determined as soon as is practicable and then *consistently* applied. Otherwise, the value of this effort will be lost, resulting in whatever seems to be the most important problem being worked on first. A lack of prioritization provides fertile ground for crisis management seeds.

Additionally, when problems have been selected by a valid ranking process, they should be satisfactorily terminated (brought to closure) before moving on to the next problem on the list. Otherwise, the concept or ranking also is voided. It should be obvious that any problem-solving organization or activity can effectively work on a finite number of problems at once. If one tries to solve problems all at once, why bother to rank them?

Selecting Candidates for Analysis

Once the problems are listed using whatever criteria has been adopted for ranking them in order of importance, the next step is to select candidates for analysis. Usually this is done in order of their rank. The only decisions left might be the resource loading or, alternately, the number of problems under consideration at any given time. Resource loading obviously is gated by available problem-solving resources and any time constraints imposed by the problem itself. The effective solution of most problems requires team effort. Some may require external assistance or other input from outside sources. Problem analysis and eventual resolution usually involve a number of separate steps. It may be possible, for example, to research one problem while working on the root cause analysis or derivation of potential solutions of another problem. Obviously this approach applies to team situations and may in fact play to the strengths of certain team members. Like all juggling acts, while impressive to watch, they also can quickly become disasters. At first, it is wise to work through problems one at a time.

There is another technique that is worth examining. Quite often, considerable likeness may be detected in the problem listing, although the rankings themselves vary. For example, "lack of adequate procedures" may be listed as apparent cause for problems ranked 3, 7, 12, 17, etc. on the list. Although this may be the apparent cause, it might be worthwhile to consider these problems together. The logic in gathering problems for analysis is that often it is the case that the same root cause has precipitated a number of similar problems. This pattern recognition may also occur during the analysis process itself, when a set of causal conditions is similar to another surfaced problem. As alluded to above, the experience factor is important in an effective root cause analysis system. After a while, one gets a feel for these things.

Selecting Analysis Techniques That Will Be Utilized
This is another aspect of the overall root cause analysis process which will continue to be refined as experience is accumulated. The good news is that any of the root cause analysis techniques described in this book should work for almost any problem.

Certain techniques, however, will tend to be easier to use than others on a particular type of problem. For example, change analysis (described in Chapter 8) is perhaps the easiest to understand and apply of the formal techniques discussed in this book. However, change analysis is difficult to use when you cannot detect what is different or has changed. With only a short time in grade, most analysts can quickly decide which of the various root cause analysis techniques is best suited for application to a given problem.

There always is some danger in suggesting which analysis technique is more appropriate except in a general sense. The specific problem to be analyzed remains the prime determinant and accumulated experience the best guide. As mentioned previously, because of their nature or structure, certain analysis techniques seem to work better given a particular situation. Table 3.1 summarizes this advice.

The assignment of the ratings of good, better, and best in Table 3.1 was done by hypothesizing a particular kind of situation. For example, in looking at what appears to be a basic organizational problem, barrier analysis, which focuses on administrative and procedural systems, would appear easiest to use, but tree diagrams also work well since they tend to display structure and relationships. Change analysis can be used and is particularly helpful if there have been recent changes or personnel turnover. In short, they all work.

Similar guidance on the choice of the more appropriate root cause analysis technique for a given problem situation is given in Figure 3.1. Once again, this is provided only as guidance as to which root cause analysis technique *might* work better under certain circumstances.

Problem Nature	Change Analysis	Barrier Analysis	Event and Causal Factors Analysis	Tree Diagrams
Organizational	Good	Best	—	Better
Activity or Process	Good	Best	Good	Better
Reorganization	Best	Good	—	Better
New or Changed Activity	Best	Better	—	Good
Personnel	Good	Best	Better	—
Accident or Incident	Good	Better	Best	Good

Table 3.1

Comparison of Analysis Techniques

Most of the questions in Figure 3.1 are self-explanatory; however, we will provide some elaboration. The first question "Consequences?" requests a response in terms of "high" or "low." This is both organization- and situation-specific. If the response is "low," another question is posed relative to the problem being a near miss in terms of being serious or catastrophic. Quite often, the problem or unwanted condition by and of itself may be minor, but luck or some ameliorating condition prevented something far worse from occurring. In this case, it may be worthwhile to provide detailed analysis.

The question of single (or first) occurrence also is important. Often we are plagued by a series of low-level problems that, in a cumulative sense, should be considered as serious. Even with a single occurrence, if the chances are high that it will occur again, the problem may warrant further consideration. If all the answers to these questions point in the right direction, then any of the less-structured techniques may be adequate.

Following the logic diagram in the other direction, the next question is one of whether or not serious injury resulted. If the answer is "yes," then MORT (see Chapter 12), with its safety and accident focus, might be

Figure 3.1
Selection of Analysis Technique

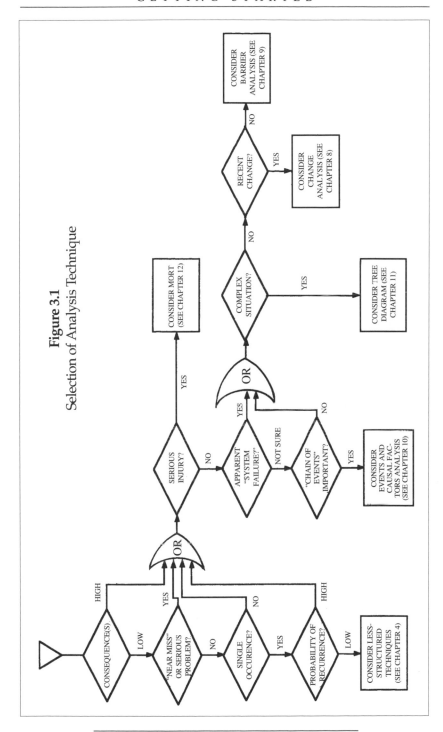

considered. The question "Apparent system failure?" refers to the administrative and organizational systems in place. If the response is "not sure," then another question is asked as to the importance of missing or chained events. If the series of events (or conditions surrounding them) appear to hold the clues, then event and causal factors analysis might be the best choice.

If there has been an apparent system failure, but the problem situation appears fairly straightforward, then either change analysis (if there has been recent change) or barrier analysis may be considered. If the problem appears more complex, then tree diagrams may be a better choice.

Organizations may choose to adopt Figure 3.1 as shown or modify it to their particular needs by inserting more specific decision nodes in the diagram. Once again, caution is advised not to focus on technique selection, except as a secondary issue.

Analysts tend to have favorite techniques. Given that the various root cause techniques (properly applied) *should* produce the same results, even though another technique might be more efficient or straightforward, it doesn't really matter. Don't take your eyes off the ball: the important thing is that you are solving problems; how you do it is of lesser importance. Leave any arguments related to inelegance of approach to the theorists. In most real-life problem situations, it will be the result (eventual solution) that will be important, not the means (analysis technique).

Pulse Points
and Validation Concepts

Whether researching a particular problem or trying to decide the best place from which to continually observe things, it becomes apparent that there are points or places that provide the clearest insight into operations/activities. Now let's borrow something learned in basic first aid. There are a number of points on the human body at which it is easiest to detect heartbeats. These are called pulse points, the most familiar one being the wrist. This same concept can be employed in organizations. Pulse points are those particular places where operations of the system are most easily evidenced; alternately, they are the points at which problems are most likely to occur.

Each firm or organization can identify these points as they are obvious once some thought is given to the concept. For example, they are the items that an experienced production foreman usually checks on rounds. He or she knows exactly what to look at that will provide the clearest idea of how things are going. The only problem may be in taking the time to think them through and set them down in a formal fashion.

Although these points may be identified through operations analysis, they are most often located through experience. Just as the seasoned production foreman does not look into every detail on these rounds, the specific items checked are those that, through accumulated experience, can be relied upon as operational indicators. It is purposive, nonrandom, focused, subjective sampling.

This is similar to the validation concepts widely used within certain industries. Validation involves checking of product quality at predetermined points during the process. For example, these techniques are routine in the pharmaceutical industry. Once the finished product is made into pills or caplets, it is either acceptable or unacceptable. Talk about the need for a zero defects program; in this case it is all or nothing. The obvious time to find discrepancies is during the process, when there may be still opportunities for corrections.

When the process or activity reaches a particular validation checkpoint and passes, it then proceeds to the next checkpoint, until it is completed. One advantage of this technique is that when these points are chosen carefully and the appropriate criteria applied, the source of any problem is easy to find.

The technique is similar to the hold or witness points familiar in manufacturing or construction. If these points are properly chosen, they are invaluable in verifying achieved quality or process/activity correctness to that point. Similar to validation measures, they should be chosen to facilitate appropriate correction before subsequent processes or activities make it difficult or impossible.

On an organizational basis, there are certain situations that might suggest the need for increased scrutiny. These include, but are not limited to:

- Changes in the management or direct supervision
- Significant increases or decreases in staffing levels
- New or substantially revised procedures
- Recent policy changes
- New or unique programs
- Changes in problem patterns

When considering developing and installing pulse points, it is better to start with as few of these checkpoints as seems appropriate to the process or activity. The number of checkpoints can always be increased later if needed. If too many checkpoints are chosen, it may introduce substantial inefficiencies for which there may be no payback. Although checking every step of certain activities or processes may be necessary, with most it is not. Remember the intent is not to inspect quality in (which cannot be done) but to verify the status of processes and activities.

The checkpoints may be shifted if needed. This might occur because the first guess was wrong or because other portions of the overall process or activity suggest closer looks are needed. Conditions could have changed over time or as new techniques were introduced. Once again, consider the borrowed term pulse points. The main idea is to identify a finite number of reliable indicators of organizational, process, or activity health, or proper functioning.

Initiating Data Inputs

The subject of data collection will be discussed in both the context of gathering appropriate data in researching a particular problem, as well as in devising needed input to an effective root cause analysis system. The collection of the necessary, related data was the scientific method's third step.

The obvious first question is "How much data is required?" The answer is "No more than is needed." This obvious answer might have been different several years ago, but now we live in what has been termed the information age. Computers are widely used to collect, store, and upon request, provide managers and analysts with data, computations, graphs, etc. Data on nearly everything is collected and stored by most organizations. Release of this vast accumulation of information without some planning can create a virtual paper tsunami.

Receiving a huge amount of information, some directly bearing on the problem, some peripheral, and most not related in any fashion, invariably will result in confusion. At the very least, more time may be spent trying to locate the needle in the haystack than in solving the problem itself. This is not to suggest that computers are to be avoided. The message, however, is to design a problem or deficiency reporting system that is usable. Start simple and keep it that way, unless it is not providing you with *most* of the information you need. Accept that computers will not give you *all* the information you need anyway. Also, unless you're careful, you can easily find yourself playing a numbers game.

One of the best suggestions that can be offered here is to start simple, then get fancy, and don't get fancy unless it is necessary.

In gathering data for a specific problem or designing needed input to a fault detection and reporting system, the following question should be asked: How well does the data collected "line up" with the problem statement and the analysis technique chosen? The idea of gathering data directly aligned with the particular aspects of the problem and analysis needs is depicted in Figure 3.2. The search for the most appropriate information and data is thereby guided and any number of false starts or re-searching for missing pieces can be avoided.

For example, if the problem statement suggests personnel or equipment failures as potential problem sources and the root cause technique chosen is barrier analysis, then the data collected should focus on missing or less than adequate safeguards. This is not to suggest that blinders be worn, but that the stimulus be that sufficient data is collected along the specific lines of inquiry. The exact amount of data needed to form accurate, defensible solutions will vary by problem and consequence, but the knack of collecting the right amount of the proper data will largely come from experience.

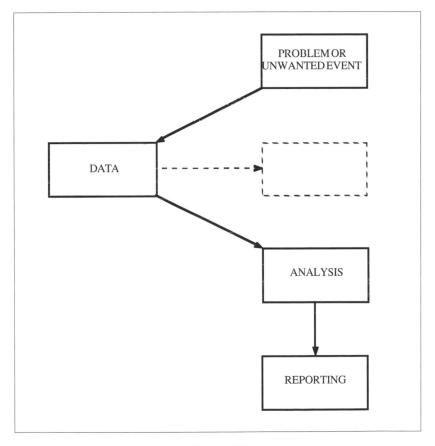

Figure 3.2
"Lining Up" the Data Input

Trend Analysis

Trend analysis is one of the most discussed and least understood analysis techniques. Trend analysis is considered by many to be an essential part of any effective corrective action system, which it cannot be, except in an indirect way. It also is often synonymous with the computerized manipulation of data into the number of problems of one type or another, the number of items for which corrective action is overdue, etc., but this is status reporting, not trend analysis.

If these are misconceptions, what then is trend analysis? The definition of trend analysis is given in any basic statistics textbook. Trend is one of the components in a time series analysis, specifically the long-term directional component. It is *not* the cyclical component (with which trend is sometimes confused), the random or chance fluctuations which occur, *nor* seasonal variation (which is seldom if ever considered, but should be).

Trend defines long-term movement or direction. Trend analysis serves as a useful input to the overall problem identification and resolution process, since it indicates this gradual direction. It tells you if you are heading in the right (or wrong) direction, but it is definitely not a detailed street map.

The problem with this general misunderstanding of trend analysis is that valid trend analysis is rarely performed. This situation results in a form of shortsightedness. Effective trend analysis gives historical perspective and shows you the direction in which you are headed. It can help you see the light at the end of a tunnel even if that light is a freight train heading straight at you. Even bad news can be helpful, however, if it gives you a chance to react in time.

Coding Causes

Almost all established root cause analysis systems include a coding or classification system for causes. According to our previous definition of the most basic reasons faults occur, this list usually will be 10 to 30 items in length. Although there can be as few as three or four root causes listed, following the logic that problems can be attributed to either people, equipment or material, or procedures, this approach does not provide the needed focus. The problem buckets are just too large and nonspecific. For example, it is difficult to work on people problems without some further idea of which aspect is of particular interest. In most coding systems, one of the root causes might be "supervision," which at least gives a better idea of the nature of the problem. Further breakdown can be provided within the supervision root cause category, such as "definition of work assignments." This is done to describe the detail under the root cause for which a more specific remedy might be needed.

Using this breakdown, the list of specific, assignable causes might be 100 to 300 items in length. These are shown as subcategories under the more generic root cause and are useful in assigning apparent causes or in later data evaluation to determine the nature of organizational problems.

With reference to the previous definitions of root and apparent causes, as well as symptoms (see Chapter 1 and Figure 1.2), the number of specific causal factors and their more generic root cause is as shown in Figure 3.3.

Another illustration of this concept might be that of progressively finer sieves. The finest mesh collects a great deal of matter, whereas the coarsest allows most of the material to pass through, collecting little. The obvious problem is to determine which mesh sieve will provide sufficient separation to allow meaningful examination. In terms of an

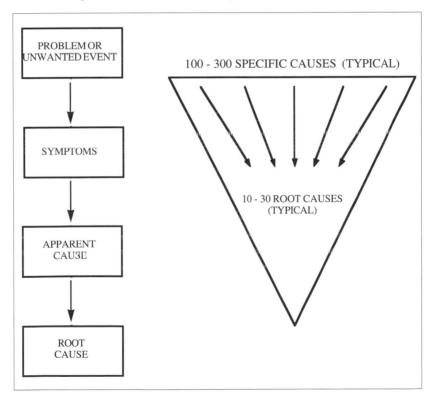

Figure 3.3
Relationship of Specific and Root Causes

organization, the mesh size is that which allows problems to be identified with suitable clarity at the root cause level.

To illustrate what a listing of root cause codes might look like, Figure 3.4 shows some typical root cause codes. These were modeled after the Institute of Nuclear Power Operations (INPO) root cause codes, which are widely used within the commercial nuclear power industry. It is recognized that these codes would have limited applicability and might require different interpretations in other industries, or the service sector. They are shown to illustrate the sort of basic groupings of root causes an organization might consider.

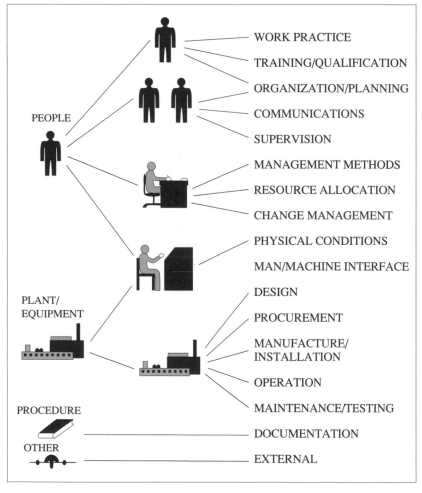

Figure 3.4
Typical Root Cause Codes

The column on the extreme left-hand side shows very basic problem cause groupings. Problems can be traced to personnel errors, material or equipment, procedures, or some other cause. The center column begins to break these broader groupings down further. For example, under people-related problems, there are other categories. The first category concerns those problems strictly associated with the individual, those related to interpersonal causes (supervision, communications, management, etc.), and finally those associated with the individual's environment (physical conditions and man–machine interface). The diagram is useful in understanding just how these causes relate to each other.

The reader is reminded of the 10–30 root causes depicted in Figure 3.3. In Figure 3.4, 17 root causes are shown. The definitions for each of these root cause categories follow.

Work Practices: Methods routinely used in the performance of a task. Included are necessary preparation, document use, equipment/material use, and practices for error detection.

Training/Qualification: Proficiency in the task assigned, including any specified qualification/certification requirements. Includes the training activity, both formal and informal, and its effectiveness.

Work Organization/Planning: Scoping, planning, organizing, and scheduling the performance of a task or activity. Includes the identification of specific resource requirements.

Communications: The presentation of information, whether spoken or written. Effectiveness is related to both content and method.

Supervision: Techniques used to direct and monitor personnel in the performance of their assigned task or activity.

Management Methods: Techniques used to provide organization, program and administrative policies, overall resource and schedule planning, direction of activities, interface with other organizations, and control and oversight of activities.

Note: The following two root causes could be considered part of management methods above, but are considered separately to allow subsequent differentiation.

Resource Allocation: The process of allocating manpower, material, or other resources, including financial, for the accomplishment of a particular task/objective. Effectiveness is related to schedule and priority considerations.

Change Management: The process of modifying/revising a particular design, operation, technique, or system. Includes both hardware and software (such as procedures, organization, document revision, etc.), as well as transition planning.

Physical Conditions: Physical and environmental conditions, equipment layout, accessibility and other factors in the work area impacting personnel or equipment performance.

Man/Machine Interface: The design and maintenance of equipment/items used to communicate information to the person (tags, labels, signs, alarms, etc.) or from the worker (controls) which impact plant/system or worker performance.

Design: The design and configuration of equipment/systems (or subsystems) required to support operations or activities. This includes initial design bases and the control of any required modifications or changes.

Procurement: The process of acquiring necessary resources, personnel, equipment, material, or systems.

Equipment Manufacture and Installation: Includes on- or off-site manufacturing/assembly of equipment, its storage and handling, up to and including its initial installation.

Plant/System Operation: The actual operation of permanently installed, temporary or portable equipment or systems in their intended function.

Maintenance/Testing: Management system and process of maintaining equipment, processes or systems in optimum condition. Includes preventive maintenance, calibration, and repairs.

Documentation: Preparation, approval, completion, distribution, control and retention of appropriate instructions, procedures, drawings, and other documentation or records of activities.

External: Influence outside the usual control of the organization. Includes requirements imposed by other agencies or organizations, weather, sabotage, etc.

Other groupings can be considered when tailoring this sample listing to a specific organization. For instance, a manufacturing firm may wish to separate material and equipment; another firm may wish to break down management methods into finer categories. Not all categories may apply. Remember that this listing was provided as typical.

Once an appropriate root cause grouping has been devised for a particular organization, the next topic that needs to be covered is how and when these cause codes will be applied. We have already alluded that faults can be fixed at the symptom or apparent cause level, but that they are more likely to be prevented by examining the more basic root cause. (Refer to the discussion of this subject in Chapter 2.) Assigned causes, however, can be of considerable value during the analysis phase as long as it is remembered what they actually represent: the initial belief of an observer or reporter who admittedly may be closer to the problem than the analyst. In assessing the value of any previously assigned cause, the analyst needs to know when and where it was applied.

Causes can be coded on problem or deficiency reports in a number of ways. They can be assigned at the problem origin. One of the pros to this approach is the included opinion of a direct or close problem or condition observer. Two of the cons include the inability to see the larger picture and the need to train a larger number of people in exactly what each code represents to achieve any sort of consistency.

Cause codes also can be applied at some intermediate point. There are advantages to this approach, which include consistency and a certain amount of detachment. Obviously, the number of personnel requiring training in the meaning of the codes is reduced. On the other hand, there is a loss in direct or close observational value and less understanding of exactly what is represented by the problem or event description.

Lastly, causes may not be coded at all, leaving this to the analysis process. As with the other approaches, this has both advantages and disadvantages. There is no easy solution to the question of where and when causes should be assigned. One of the major disadvantages of coding causes, regardless of when they are applied, is that cause coding can end up as a substitute for effective evaluations. It becomes easy to resort to tallies of assigned causes as a substitute for an effective root cause analysis program. It has been the authors' personal experience that, even with a relatively simple coding system, two qualified and otherwise competent analysts will agree on an apparent cause call only 80 percent of the time. When these calls are based solely on a written problem or event description and the necessary field work or investigation is conducted, fully 50 percent of these initial calls may later be revised.

What have been the lessons learned so far? One important lesson is that when devising a cause coding system, the number of selections should be kept at a minimum. Another lesson is that recognition be given that these coded causes can only be considered as the apparent causes until the root cause analysis confirms them to be correct. Finally that, regardless of the number of causes listed, bias may be present. Coded causes should be viewed the same as any other input, subject to verification based on understood limitations. The tabulation of coded causes should never be substituted for a true root cause evaluation process. Personnel will need training, not just in the use of the codes, but in understanding the problem identification and resolution system they represent.

Avoiding the Trivial Pursuit™ Game

Almost everyone is familiar with this popular game. It is based on successfully answering questions on trivia, defined by Webster as "unimportant matters." In terms of an effective root cause analysis program, it can be a serious drawback. Remember the saying of not being able to spot the forest because of the trees. In data gathering, as well as the subsequent analysis phase, this is a common trap.

Because it is an easy trap to fall into, the best hope is that only efficiency will suffer. A darker outcome would be obscuring the real cause of problems. Support personnel, particularly those assigned to the computer department or others with that particular interest, will be happy to oblige if you wish to play this game. It probably is true that whatever data you deem important can be captured. It also is true that this data, once obtained, can then be combined, ratioed, tallied, and graphed, as you wish.

It is a comfortable approach. Most people feel secure in their own little corners, with facts with which they are familiar, with their routine. Concentrating on the trivial aspects or details is satisfying, or at least not demanding. All of this would be only mildly interesting if it did not routinely result in management reports that contain so much trivial detail that they are virtually useless, or in analysis reports that identify only the tip of the iceberg (or possibly even the wrong one as the result of a confused analysis).

How can this trap be avoided? Obviously, don't start collecting more information than you need to start. If this advice is a little late, then note which sources or data you refer to normally. Once you have a fair idea of what you really need, eliminate the rest (that's right, eliminate). Take yourself off the distribution of reports you never use. Be more specific about data you request. Try leaving important "stuff" in your IN basket for a while. This may make you a little nervous at first but if it is important, you'll find out quickly enough. When your boss asks why you haven't gotten to it yet, it will give you the opportunity to post him or her on all the things you do and how busy you are. If you don't hear anything, chances are the important "stuff" wasn't that important after all. (Yes, Virginia, there is such a thing as corporate junk mail.)

Test your output channels, too. Take a critical look at what you produce. Do you think someone really needs this or have you also become a junk mailer? If in doubt, simply ask the recipient (be prepared for some surprises). Ask others what is important and what is not. If you want to justify your efforts and make it sound important, call it basic requirements analysis or information systems engineering.

Everyone has become an information junkie to some extent. The important task is to find a way to separate the important from the trivial.

Given limited processing time, it's not just a means of improving our performance, it's an imperative. Avoid the pursuit of trivia.

Confounding Effects and Other Problems

The term *confounding* is borrowed from mathematics. Simply stated, it means that some unknown or unrecognized influence is causing an effect. The best example of confounding effects is the famous Hawthorne Study.

Conducted during the late 1920s as part of the developing industrial engineering discipline, it took place at the Hawthorne plant owned by Western Electric in Cicero, Illinois. The study followed classical experiment guidelines. Both an experimental and control group were formed. The purpose was to determine the effects of various factors on production (e.g., heating and lighting). In consultation with the experimental group, lighting was increased. This resulted in improved production. Other factors were dealt with similarly. In every case, when one of these factors was improved, increased production also resulted. The study team was elated. The industrial engineers felt they had identified a number of factors which, if improved, would result in increased production. It was only a matter of writing up the report and forwarding it to management.

Then, whether deliberately or not, it was decided to return each of the factors to their original condition. This would verify the results as the expected drop in production occurred. Once again, in consultation with the experimental group, they decided to reduce the lighting. Unpredictably, however, production rose again. Each time another factor was changed, this unexpected result occurred. The team finally realized that an unseen (confounding) factor was present. Readers who have followed this story so far know what that factor is: employee involvement in decision making. This was later incorporated as one element in programs such as quality circles, as well as the more current TQM concepts.

The failure to recognize confounding or hidden effects can lead to catastrophic conclusions. For example, suppose a company decided on a performance indicator of "defects/100 production units," or "defects/100 man-hours." This ratio (and it should be recognized as such) can be influenced by a change in either the numerator or the denominator, or both. Conversely, appropriate changes in both can cause the indicator to appear stable or unchanging.

The performance indicator does not address differences in the design of production units or their complexity. It does not address turnover in personnel, nor the lack of any required training. It does not address particular problems with a batch of raw materials or parts. The cautions could continue. It is mentioned here only to point out the problem of hidden or confounding effects in data and analysis.

One fact that emerges is that most indicators or tallies of data usually require some interpretation. Otherwise, they may suggest problems when none exist. Throughout this book, this same basic caution will be provided. Blind reliance on purely mechanical measures should be avoided. All of these tools may be extremely useful, but caution is urged in their use.

Training Personnel

Which personnel will require training in root cause analysis techniques? Obviously, those personnel who may be involved in performing root cause analyses need training in the techniques and their use. Beyond these personnel, however, others responsible for identifying and describing problems also will need training to help understand their role in the overall improvement process. First-line supervisors and managers, the users of the final analysis product, also will need training in their use, as well as developing an understanding that effective fault identification and resolution makes sense in the long run.

Total quality management concepts emphasize broad participation in the decision-making process as well as the value of team effort. Taking this philosophy, it becomes apparent that *all* personnel require some training. Certainly top management must be made aware of (and support) any quality and productivity program, but the simple fact that emerges is: *The identification and resolution of problems is everyone's responsibility.*

Summary

As the reader progresses through this book, it will become apparent that a subtitle might have been *A Primer on Effective Problem Solving.* Root cause analysis is one of the tools used in this process. Effective root cause analyses are highly dependent on the input data utilized. It is important to gather all relevant data, but it also is important to avoid overloading the system or analysis with extraneous or trivial information. The analyst must be constantly aware of hidden factors, which influence the analysis and could obscure the real cause. Although coding of faults can be of some value, care must be used in their interpretation and use. Perhaps more importantly, the root cause analysis effort cannot be reduced to a numbers game.

Effective quality and productivity programs require that all personnel understand its purpose, develop an awareness of the objectives and interest in making it work, and eventually assume a participative position.

4

ROOT CAUSE ANALYSIS
TECHNIQUES

"Now 'tis the spring, and weeds are shallow-rooted;
Suffer them now and they'll o'ergrow the garden."
— William Shakespeare, 1564-1616,
King Henry VI

Introduction

This chapter provides an overview of some of the methods (analysis techniques) that are used in root cause analysis. There are a large number of root cause analysis techniques available. The first problem might seem to be which technique to choose. The available root cause analysis techniques range from relatively simple, unstructured approaches to the more elaborate, formal evaluation methods, such as management oversight and risk tree analysis (MORT), discussed in Chapter 12.

One of the important concepts provided in this book is the graded approach to root cause analysis. Adoption of a graded approach will greatly influence the analysis method selected. Simply stated, the graded approach suggests that the analysis (and subsequent level of corrective or preventive actions taken) fit the problem, event, or undesirable

---

condition. The graded approach to root cause analysis should be dictated by risk management considerations. Risk management implies that the appropriate amount and rigor of the analysis is consistent with the assessed impact of the problem or its recurrence on the organization. This means that, among other criteria, the depth, scope, and focus of analysis efforts will be influenced by the magnitude of the potential loss (or level of impairment imposed by the condition) as well as the undesirability of a recurrence. It would seem unnecessary to perform an elaborate root cause analysis on a relatively straightforward problem which leads to minimum operational impact. Conversely, other problems definitely would require detailed and careful analysis; this class of faults has been termed *show-stoppers.*

This chapter will present some basically unstructured as well as structured but less formal techniques that can be used to effectively determine the root cause of problems, events, or unwanted conditions. Subsequent chapters will discuss some of the more formal root cause analysis techniques.

Introductory Story

This book is about effective problem solving—working smarter, not harder. It is about fixing problems once and for all. The following introductory story about problem solving is true. The only thing changed is the person's name; we will call him Clark Wayne.

After all these years, I still believe Clark Wayne was one of the more clever persons I have ever known. At least it seemed so at the time I knew him. He's gone now and perhaps time has polished the memories. My experience with Clark took place when I was a recently graduated engineer, full of book knowledge, just beginning my career as a design engineer in a high-volume electronics manufacturing plant. Clark was a floor engineer.

For those unfamiliar with the production environment, a floor engineer represents the engineering department on the manufacturing line. It is the floor engineer's responsibility, for example, to oversee prototype production, examine first run assemblies, make on-the-spot design changes if needed, give feedback to the design engineers on manufacturability, and provide technical support to the production foremen and other manufacturing personnel. In short, the floor engineer does whatever is needed.

Whenever a problem arose (and they often did), everyone turned to Clark for a solution. Since he had been in design for many years and then immersed in the production process ever since, he seemed to have a store of knowledge that provided just the right solution every time, whether it was an obviously needed design change, material substitution, improved assembly technique, or whatever.

Less Structured Approaches

From the introductory story, it should be recognized that effective problem solving is not inextricably tied to formal root cause analysis techniques. Clark Wayne, based on his accumulated experience and the ability to apply this knowledge, was considered an effective problem solver. I've met other people since then who seem to exhibit the same characteristics. In retrospect, why these people were effective seems simple. For one thing, they knew their business. They knew the right questions to ask. They were able to take the current problem or condition and relate it to others which were similar in some way, devise a number of trial solutions, choose the best, test it and make modifications if that didn't work. They appeared to be able to recognize patterns from fragments and have the ability to determine which pieces were needed to provide sufficient information on which to make a decision. Lastly, they were willing to make a decision and accept the consequences if they were wrong. This last trait seems most important and a key factor in successful problem resolution. Fear of failure can be paralyzing. Consciously or not, many organizations punish failure to the extent that the natural response evoked in most personnel is to cover their tails and do little more than is expected.

The same traits that Clark displayed ensure success for a detective, investigative reporter, auto mechanic, internist, etc. There are a number of activities and professions for which the requirement for success is a combination of logical thinking, experience, and intuition. Experience from which learning occurs can be attained only through exposure and an innate inclination to learn. Applying lessons learned from experience therefore involves both attitude and discipline. Logic can be refined and polished. The use of purely intuitive thinking in decision making can be reinforced by the inclusion of hard facts and data in the process.

Although intuitive thinking ability seems to be a personal characteristic, these traits may be improved through training or education, as well as practice and experience. Some persons seem to be naturally effective problem solvers, others are not. Of the latter group, some can be trained. The remainder may never be effective, regardless of what is done. Few people like problems, although some people seem to enjoy the challenge of solving them. If your organization has a few people who seem to find satisfaction in solving problems, encourage their efforts.

Reward their successes and overlook their failures—they can't be right all the time. Meanwhile, faults are being corrected and prevented. This environment will almost be an imperative if the organization is to remain competitive. Few firms can maintain the burden imposed by unresolved problems, which manifests itself in increased scrap or rework, less than adequate finished quality, excessive overhead costs, and so on.

Some Unstructured Methods

It is easier to discuss some of the less-structured root cause analysis techniques and then proceed to the more formal techniques. Being less structured should not be interpreted as being less valid. Many of the less formal techniques presented herein may provide as legitimate a solution as a more formal technique. Some of the less structured root cause analysis methods include:

- Intuition
- Networking
- Experience
- Other semistructured approaches

All of the above techniques may be utilized for root cause analyses, but it should be pointed out that they have a greater degree of *subjectivity* than some of the more formal methods discussed in the following chapters. For the same reason, these techniques evidence less repeatability, the ability of one analyst to replicate the work of another. This fact must be recognized during any evaluation process.

Intuition

It might seem odd to find a discussion of intuition in a book of this type. Nonetheless, we already have established that this concept of the native ability to solve problems can be effective. Intuition is defined as "the immediate knowing or learning of something without the conscious use of reasoning; instantaneous apprehension."

The lack of the conscious use of reasoning in the above definition would seem to be a fatal flaw in our argument, but in reality the approach is the basis for a serious branch of philosophy. The philosophy of intuitionism states that the reality of perceived objects can be known only through intuition. Let us continue with the explanation.

Quite often, in analyzing an event or condition, many of the circumstances or causes are veiled. They do not surface directly; their influence is hidden. Perceptions may be the only evidence, albeit intangible. Intuitionism, however, states that their reality or existence can be known by intuition. It has been the authors' experience that, after several root cause analysis seminars, engineers, and managers often will remark that they somehow knew all along that intuition was part of the problem solving process. Trained for so many years in exact, quantifiable analysis methods, they had still maintained their belief that intuition also was important and were relieved to have this confirmed.

Unfortunately, accurate intuition seems to be a highly personal trait. Some individuals seem to immediately sense what the problem or its cause is. Others do not and may never possess this sense. There is some mental process taking place which will never be fully understood until the basic thought process itself is fully understood. The human brain is by far the most complex computer imaginable. No one really knows how it works, but most agree that it processes information in a far different fashion than digital computers. Even expert systems require the considerable assistance of this more powerful machine to work. Two of the important operating aspects of the human mind that will be examined here are its ability to detect a low-level signal in background noise and the ability to form abstract conclusions.

Detecting Low-Level Signals in Noise

One of the difficulties in instrumentation is the detection of low-level signals in background noise. There are a number of sophisticated techniques that have been devised to accomplish this, but the human mind appears to be able to accomplish this with little difficulty, almost automatically. For example, consider a mother who hears the faint cries of her baby over the noise of the TV, other children playing, the dog barking, and other noise. Another example might be the routine drive to work or home. Have you ever considered how much conscious thinking was required? The mind seems to take care of the numerous instructions and commands that would represent a major programming effort for a digital computer. It does all of this while processing a myriad of other inputs and outputs such as listening to the radio and conducting conversations with passengers. Yet, if something is different or wrong, it immediately processes a priority interrupt message. The fact that you missed a turn flashes to the conscious mind. Or, you are suddenly drawn to the fact that a ladder is against a house which wasn't there yesterday. Of all the visual input the mind has received and processed, why was that one (perhaps relatively minor) bit of information immediately brought to your attention?

In problem solving, this same process occurs. In assembling the facts, the mind somehow focuses on what otherwise might appear to be an insignificant detail. It may ultimately be this piece of the puzzle that makes the rest sensible. Seemingly unimportant clues are the stuff of great detective novels. Accept the fact that your mind is sending you a message that, for whatever reason, it is having trouble processing or wants more detail on a missing piece. If something occurs to you during the conduct of an investigation or analysis, *write it down*. The question may be answered later or with the eventual discovery of harder data or facts, but that's OK. Otherwise you may overlook an important piece of the puzzle, one that eventually might help all the rest make sense. Trust your intuition.

Formation of Abstract Conclusions
Another feature associated with human thinking is the ability to form abstract conclusions. Here we interpret this as the ability to come to a conclusion that does not follow the obvious straight line destination suggested by the accumulated facts. This conclusion may be more accurate than those suggested by formal logic. Abstract reasoning is an intricate process of cause and effect relationships. As with the later discussion of events and causal factors, these linkages will require some testing. The important point presented here, however, is that often the mind can see the real cause for a problem or unwanted condition, whereas a more formal root cause analysis technique will give the more mechanical or logical answer. Although the latter may not be wrong, it may be less incisive.

Abstract thinking can also disclose the reason behind the reason. For example, many of the recent railroad disasters have been traced to drug or alcohol abuse. The obvious solution might be screening or emphasis of the rules, but the real cause may be embedded more deeply. The daily routine of a train engineer or conductor is one of considerable boredom, with long periods of inactivity. Job rules require that they be in a certain location, although there is little to do. Perhaps different work scheduling or loading might help. The reader also is invited to think through other possible solutions to change the work environment itself, thereby mitigating or hopefully eliminating the cause of these problems. The point is that this abstract thinking, not *directly* suggested by the problem, may ultimately provide the most meaningful long-term solution. In thinking through problems and solutions, it often is helpful to let your mind freewheel for a time. This can produce unexpected but welcome results.

Networking

Networking, a current vogue, is defined as the informal communication system between individuals with similar interests. Currently, it is in vogue in any number of areas. Networking also is a potentially effective technique for problem solving. Networking can be the process used for dissemination of lessons learned.

One of the methods in solving problems that might be considered is to talk with others who might have similar problems or, preferably, not only had them but successfully solved them. It seems extremely inefficient to repeat the entire analysis and solution development process every time the same problem occurs, but many organizations do exactly this. The word does not get around. One facility, branch, or organization will experience the same problem that others did. It is a costly communications breakdown.

Some companies have adopted a formal system for disseminating lessons learned or information on potentially generic problems. Although many of these problems may not repeat or surface elsewhere, the system is paid for by the few that don't because of adequate warning. It's inexpensive fault protection insurance. Admit your problem/failure for the rest of the organization's benefit.

How can you establish a networking system? In an informal sense, it's as simple as picking up your phone and calling a peer. Describe your problem and ask for any suggestions. Ask if similar problems or conditions are evidenced elsewhere. Talk shop now and then with others. See if you can draw out discussion. Pay attention when others are talking about their problems; they may be related to, or eventually become, yours.

A more formal approach can be a Problem Report or similar system which distributes information on real or suspected problems to all cognizant and interested personnel. The system may solicit responses and suggestions or request that recipients identify similar problems. Using an iterative process, these responses may then be recirculated on an informational or action basis. It's amazing how easily a system such as this can be established. In the nuclear power industry, these formal systems are used extensively. This is partly due to the widespread criticism that lessons learned during the construction or operation of one plant were not disseminated to others. The stated aim is to avoid repeating the same problems. The more objective this process and the more willing participants become to share this information, obviously the more successful it will be. As someone laconically observed: "Networking works."

Experience

Experience can be an effective means of root cause analysis. Although there is considerable subjectivity in this approach, it can work extremely well, particularly if you have a few people like Clark Wayne. It should be obvious that the experience discussed herein has some relationship to the problems at hand, however vague or tenuous the connection might be.

Not enough credit is given to experience. Perhaps it is symptomatic of our society. Other societies place great value upon their elders, deferring to their judgment in many matters. Unlike other subject matter, experience cannot be taught; it can only be learned.

At the risk of appearing to live in the past, the author offers another true example. Several years ago, I was supervisor of a quality engineering group which, among other things, produced periodic trend and status reports for a number of large construction projects. One of the work processes that was tracked and reported upon was welding. Welding is classified as a special process, since the outcome is greatly influenced by the welder's skill. The process also is influenced by the type of material to be welded, accessibility, position (e.g. overhead welding is more difficult than welding on a bench), and other factors. One of the nonprocess factors is supervision.

It was only after some thought and experience with the welding process that reliable performance indicators were derived. Indicators, such as those routinely used in economics, are considered either lagging (after the fact), current, or leading (predictive). Of particular interest are, of course, those indicators that could be considered leading, since this allowed correction before faults surfaced. One leading indicator that was identified for the welding process was the control of weld electrodes or rods. Inadequate control of these weld rods not only could result in bad welds, but it also indicated less than adequate supervision. In relating this story, most of what has been stated seems painfully obvious, but the point is that it represented a continuing trial and error process: that process broadly termed experience.

Experience gives valuable lessons, even though some of them can be costly. Unfortunately, not everyone learns from these lessons, nor recognizes the process as one of a learning opportunity. In this situation, it is unlikely then that any lessons learned through experience will be applied.

Expert Review Teams

One of the more formal ways the experience approach to problem solving is utilized is in the formation and use of expert review teams. This is commonly done at the facility level, but it can be applied on a broader scale as well. Corporate management may even have standing committees formed of grey beards and mossbacks to provide needed independent, considered input to decisions.

Since the expert team concept is based on accumulated experience, the success or failure of this approach lies in the membership and selection criteria. Properly done, the results can be outstanding based upon the collective experience that can be focused on a particular problem. It is advisable to have the widest representation possible on these teams to avoid a narrowly focused solution. Depending upon the problem, the team might consist of an operations expert, a maintenance expert, a human performance expert, safety and quality experts, and other technical experts from engineering, procurement, research and development, construction, or manufacturing.

Other Less-Structured Approaches

Less-structured approaches are defined as those that are not recognized as formal root cause analysis techniques. This category can include a number of approaches that, in fact, are highly structured, although their original design purpose did not include determining the root cause of problems. These techniques can be extremely useful, bridging the gap from the basically unstructured techniques discussed above to the more formal, accepted root cause analysis techniques discussed in later chapters.

Some of these techniques include the following:
- PERT, CPM, or other time-event networks
- Flowcharts or process charts
- Process control charts
- Trend analyses
- Pareto diagrams
- Nominal group techniques
- Brainstorming

All of the above techniques, as well as others that might occur to the reader, may aid in the identification or visualization of the problem, event or undesired condition, or the events and conditions that led to or influenced it. They aid in the thought process. By utilizing one of these techniques, unique insight may be gained. In other cases, they may be useful in determining where else to look. For example, fishbone diagrams, flowcharts, and time-event networks are useful since they result in a picture of the process or activity. Group-think exercises, such as brainstorming and nominal group methods, help bring a collective thought process to bear on the situation and often result in novel, perhaps otherwise unnoticed solutions. On the other hand, these techniques also can result in least common denominator solutions, those minimally acceptable to all the participants. (Remember the saying that a camel was a horse designed by a committee.)

The point is that there are any number of techniques which may be used or adapted to aid problem solving. While not officially recognized as root cause analysis techniques, many of these other methods work extremely well. There is more than one way to skin a cat. What will be seen to be most important is that the problem is solved or the undesirable condition eliminated. People will probably care less about how it was done, but that it was done. This is a good example of the case in which the end justifies the means.

Some Questions

The following set of questions is offered for the reader's use in devising guidelines for problem inquiries. The list should be considered as a starting point and other questions specific to your organization can be added. What is important is that these and other questions eventually become part of your thought process when approaching problems.

1. **What really happened?** Quite often, the problem is mis-stated obscured, or the real fault is disguised. This ensures that you are working on the right problem.

2. **What was the damage or consequence?** Once again, as in Question 1, the effects may be camouflaged. It is not unusual for the effect of a problem to be understated.

3. **What was different or changed?** This may give insight into why the fault occurred, particularly with the first occurrence of a problem.

4. **What was the effect?** Studying the effect of the problem may yield clues as to its real nature and source.

5. **What might have prevented its occurrence?** This may give clues as to the systematic or program elements that were less than adequate.

6. **What really went wrong?** This question is similar to Question 1, but the focus here is not on the *what* but the *why*.

7. **Did people do what they were supposed to do?** The answer here might be difficult to obtain if the organizational climate is wrong, but the answers can point to problems in systems, training, etc.

8. **Did any event/action prevent an even worse situation?** This information is particularly useful in thinking through solutions to the problem as well as current problems in procedures, training, etc.

9. **Did people know what to do?** Somewhat like Question 7, the answer points to holes in present systems if they didn't. Although personnel can't be trained or procedures provided for all possible situations, since the fault occurred, it should have at least been considered plausible.

10. **Has this happened before?** Perhaps this should be the first question. The answer gives vital information regarding the nature of the problem as well as the efficacy of any previous corrective, adaptive, and preventive actions taken.

11. **What was done before to fix it, if anything?** The response to this question could result in an organizational "Oops."

12. **Who reported this?** Often this is important and may give clues as to problems with the reporting system itself. Was the person who reported the fault the one who should have first noticed it? Make sure that you talk to this person.

13. **What might prevent it from happening again?** This is not an attempt to jump over the analysis phase to potential solutions, but input along these lines should be held to ensure all possible fixes are eventually considered. Quite often suggested solutions obtained from close to the problem source will be the best.

Advantages/Disadvantages

Before proceeding to a discussion of the more formal root cause analysis techniques, the advantages as well as the disadvantages of the methods presented so far will be listed. The advantages include the following.

Short turnaround: Most of the techniques described thus far are generally faster in terms of solving problems than the ones described in later chapters. This can be a decided advantage when a quick answer is what is really needed.

Ability to detect low-level signals: Once again, in a general sense, the less-structured approaches provide greater ability to detect hidden issues. This capability is less in the more methodical, cookbook approach used in the more formal root cause analysis techniques

Abstract conclusions: The less-structured techniques allow the formation of conclusions which are more abstract, although this does not imply they are less valid.

The disadvantages to these techniques include the following.

Subjectivity: Most of these methods involve a great deal of subjectivity. Although this is part of their strength, it also is their weakness. The ability to replicate the process always is an issue.

Hard to train: Most of the unstructured or less-structured techniques are highly correlated to factors such as experience and intuition. Clearly these factors are the domain of inherent personality and native ability rather than subjects that can be taught in a classroom.

Requires familiarity with process: All the techniques discussed require detailed understanding of the particular process or activity. The techniques discussed in later chapters will offset this condition by their methodology.

Potential for higher probability of failure: It must be admitted that, given all the conditions needed for success with these methods, there is an increased likelihood that they may fail to arrive at the root cause of problems. If all the conditions are right, however, they can be equally effective.

Structured Approaches

As was mentioned earlier, there are a large number of structured techniques which have been developed for root cause analysis. Presentation of all these methods would require several volumes. Fortunately, many of these methods are similar. Therefore, it is possible to discuss several of the more basic types and allow the now-informed reader to discover the subtleties or variations of these basic methods. Accordingly, the basic formal root cause analysis techniques are presented in Chapters 8-12.

Advantages/Disadvantages

The advantages and disadvantages of the formal, structured approaches above may be given in a composite sense. Some of the advantages include the following.

Process definition: Each of the techniques produces some form of logic table or flow diagram. This aids in understanding the process or activity and may be of later use in correcting flaws.

Repeatability: The methods follow step-by-step procedures, which aid greatly in following what was done. In addition, it is likely that independent analysts will produce the same results. Replication usually is not a problem.

Better documentation: Generally speaking, the overall documentation produced is better. This may be particularly important in certain types of investigations—for example, those that might result in litigation.

Available literature: There exists considerable current literature on most of the formal, structured techniques.

Some of the disadvantages of the more formal techniques include the following.

Training requirements: Analysts need training in these techniques and their use. Although many of the formal root cause analysis techniques are more or less cookbook in their approach, training in their selection, use, and interpretation is required. In certain situations, accident investigators and root cause analysts *must* be certified.

Options limited by process: As has already been mentioned, the event, problem, condition, or circumstances surrounding it will, to some extent, dictate or limit the analysis technique chosen. For example, it is difficult to use change analysis when the existence or degree of change cannot be easily determined.

Outcomes influenced by method: This is the inverse of the above disadvantage. There is a built-in assumption in barrier analysis, for example, that the event or problem was caused by missing or less than adequate safeguards or barriers designed to prevent it from happening. It is most likely that the final cause will be related to these features, since this is the basis of the analysis technique used.

Bias introduced by structure: In some of the more elaborate techniques, such as MORT, the choices are deliberately limited. To the extent that all possible choices are included, this may not be a problem. It is important, however, to realize that the analysis is guided, as on a path. It is possible that not all needed paths exist or that important facts may not be discovered if they happen to be off the path.

Other advantages or disadvantages may also occur to the reader. Some of these will be more or less important depending upon the reader's particular situation or organization. There is no attempt here to persuade anyone that the more formal, structured root cause analysis techniques are somehow better than the less structured ones, or vice versa. The proper choice of root cause technique depends on the problem, its magnitude, and the consequences of its recurrence.

Correlation of Results

In many problem or accident situations, the initial choice of root cause analysis technique is important. For example, this choice may be the source of argument or exposure in subsequent litigation. Quite often, given this situation or based on risk or the potential consequence of recurrence, organizations will require that *two* different techniques be used and the results compared. This minimizes the treatment effect as well as establishes the validity of the results. It constitutes a proof in mathematical terms. Rather than rechecking the results using the same method, an entirely different technique is used.

Summary

This chapter introduced readers to the various root cause analysis techniques. There are a number of unstructured and less-structured methods that can be used for problem solving as well as the more structured root cause analysis techniques that will be covered in later chapters.

A *graded approach* to problem analysis is recommended. The effort expended in analysis should properly fit the problem, its magnitude, and the implications of its recurrence. This graded approach requires that a wide inventory of techniques be held available for use. This chapter has provided insight into some of the less formal analysis techniques that may be contemplated.

In certain situations, the results obtained using one technique may be used to correlate the findings obtained by another. This may be required in the case of serious problems or accidents.

By now the reader may have the impression that root cause analysis is as much an art as it is a science. Given the wide range of techniques that are available for solving problems, there is some virtuosity involved in the practice. The outcome, however, is what is really important, the clear identification of the real reasons that faults occur. If analyses are performed in a cursory fashion or the results generally disregarded, the overall results probably will be unimpressive. If done properly, however, root cause analysis will identify the *real* cause of problems or undesirable conditions. If you do not want to hear the answer, simply don't ask the question.

5
DEVELOPING SOLUTIONS

"Like watermen, who look astern, while they row the boat ahead."

—Plutarch, 46-120 A.D.,

Whether 'Twas Rightfully Said, Lives Concealed

Introduction

Once the overall analysis process is completed and the root cause of the event or problem has been identified, the next step normally taken is to devise potential solutions. This chapter will discuss the process of developing these potential solutions; the next chapter will discuss a number of techniques that may be used to evaluate them.

Webster's *New Twentieth Century Dictionary* (unabridged) defines "solution" as "the act, method, or process of solving a problem." In this chapter, we will consider the act itself: how people view, approach, and solve problems. We also will examine the method or process used in problem solving.

Personal Differences in Problem Solving

The importance of objectivity in determining the circumstances of an event or problem, as well as collecting appropriate information and other evidence, has been emphasized throughout this book. The root cause analysis techniques presented were designed to minimize bias and other errors attributable to subjective choices or determinations that may influence the results. The process of developing solutions is far more flexible and the constraints are fewer. Therefore, when developing solutions to a problem, the degree of subjectivity which enters into or limits the number or the value of any proposed solution(s) *must* be considered. We will examine the process in order to better understand it and thereby recognize these limits. After all, everyone has their own favorite remedy for a cold and, in their own context, they seem to work equally well.

Developing solutions to problems can be regarded as focused thinking. Thinking should be focused on the problem at hand and its probable cause, as well as the means that might be employed to reduce, avoid, mitigate, or prevent recurrence (potential solutions).

According to psychologists, an individual's quality of thinking is directly proportional to their ability to

■ Represent various aspects of the situation by symbols or concepts

■ Develop new relationships and meanings

■ Manipulate and/or organize these meanings

■ Synthesize the results in the form of rational conclusions

The process of thinking ranges between two extremes: 1) *reasoning,* which is highly directed and focused, and 2) *autistic,* which is largely self-directed and imaginative. When developing potential solutions to an event or problem, a thinking process that covers the entire range between these two extremes will provide the greatest variety of potential answers, from the most obvious to the most creative.

Depending on their background, experience, and personality, most people think in a usual, predictable manner somewhere within this range (reasoning to autistic), and generally tend to come up with a particular solution or set of answers unique to their point of reference. Recognizing these individual differences in the manner we approach problems is important, particularly when developing potential solutions. To provide balance or a wider range of possible solutions, other personnel may be solicited for input. In a group setting, brainstorming can be used to collect any number of possible solutions.

When this gathering of additional input is not practical nor possible, then the problem solver may wish to examine his/her individual tendency and then attempt to provide some compensation to this bias by deliberately jotting down other ideas without allowing the (usual) internalized evaluation process to occur first. The results often can be enlightening and might even lead to a tendency of developing a wider range of possible solutions in the future. Some guidance on cultivating alternative solutions is provided later in this chapter.

Method and Process

No discussion of solving problems would be complete without a discussion of the scientific method. The basic scientific method is as follows:
1. Define the problem.
2. Formulate a hypothesis.
3. Gather appropriate data.
4. Test the hypothesis.
5. Develop conclusions.

The basic scientific method can be restated in terms of some basic steps used in developing solutions:
1. Become familiar with all the aspects of the problem and its cause.
2. Derive a number of tentative solutions.
3. Assemble as much detail as is needed to clearly define what it will require to implement these solutions.
4. Evaluate the suggested solutions.
5. Objectively test and revise the solutions.
6. Develop a final list of potential solutions.

Some Pitfalls

The following are some of the more common pitfalls which should be avoided during any constructive problem-solving process. The list is far from complete, but is provided so that the reader will recognize and avoid these traps. To aid in accomplishing this, some remedies are also included.

Binary Thinking: This trap can be described as the failure to recognize that often there are grades or degrees of correctness represented in most solutions, as opposed to a binary (two states or conditions) right or wrong decision.

Remedies: Remember that most solutions have *some* value; it's just that some have more than others. Although all roads may lead to Rome, some are a little longer or more difficult. Perhaps with some minor modification, an idea that was destined for the junk pile may end up as the best choice.

Incomplete or Faulty Information: This pitfall is encountered when a person fails to consider all the facts or recognize that the information provided may be incomplete or inadequate. It can also occur when faults in the information are not detected, which is particularly easy to do when the information seems to fit. This corresponds to the Type II error in decision making, that of accepting facts to be true when, in fact, they are not.

Remedies: Take *nothing* for granted. Assume, until you are satisfied, that there may be something missing, something you *should* know but haven't yet been told. Be suspicious. Examine the facts, sort out the ones of which you are absolutely sure, and put the rest on this pile only when you're satisfied. Use the same thought process you would use if buying a used car from someone you don't know.

Desire to Believe: This can be evidenced by a predisposition toward certain facts or conclusions based solely on psychological values or beliefs, regardless of the evidence to the contrary. This pitfall also includes foregone conclusions, self-fulfilling prophecies, generalizations, stereotypes, and rigid preconceptions.

Remedies: Become a fact agnostic. Accept nothing except that it is proven or can be observed. Constantly check your thinking for these predeterminations; if the solution was "what you always knew it should have been," you may have already fallen into this trap.

Failure to Develop Alternate Hypotheses: This happens when a person attempts to explain all facts using a particular cause and thereby fails to consider alternate explanations or relationships. This can occur for some of the reasons listed above under "Desire to Believe," or because other solutions do not occur to you. See also "Binary Thinking."

Remedies: Disengage your mind clutch and freewheel mentally for a while. Look sideways and see if anything else appears. Walk away from the problem for a while, stare at the ceiling, or whatever, and then return to the problem. Get a fresh perspective. Ask yourself questions; ask others for their perspective as well.

Making the Pieces Fit the Puzzle: False conclusions may be appear to be consistent with the whole. This trap is encountered most often when a predetermined or preferred solution is used to influence its own development.

Remedies: Check your logic path. Does it proceed smoothly from point A to point B, all the way to point N? Is there anything that is obviously missing? Check that you have all the facts.

Correlation vs. Causation: The fact that two (or more) things *seem* to be related to each other does not mean that in fact they are. They may, in fact, be influenced by yet another, perhaps as yet unknown, factor(s).

Remedies: The fact that a train leaves the station every time the clock strikes eight o'clock does not mean that the clock striking causes the train to leave. This cause and effect problem is a big one for philosophers, too, so don't feel too bad. Try the relationship in the following sentence: It is *obvious,* even to the most casual observer, that A *must* cause B. If it doesn't sound even remotely obvious (even to you), try another cause.

Technical Terminology: Technical terminology often is used to cover cloudy thinking. Buzz words also can create misunderstanding, particularly if their meaning is obscure and therefore subject to the interpretation of others.

Remedies: Do some serious proofreading. Remember the adage: Keep it simple! Try your response on someone totally unfamiliar with your discipline or area of interest. Then ask them to tell you what you just told them. Listen to their answer.

Words vs. Meaning: Similar in some respects to the previous trap, this is the failure to recognize the considerable difference in meaning and sense that different people will attribute to the same word or symbol. This problem was eloquently described in Alvin Toffler's best-seller *Future Shock*. Toffler described cultural shock experienced by Peace Corps volunteers when they found certain actions or responses could have the opposite meaning in a different culture.

Remedies: Similar to buzz words, this pitfall is a little harder to detect. The remedy, however, is the same. Make sure everyone understands what you really mean.

Not Checking Thinking and Opinions: Accepting the first or more obvious solutions, failing to seek and consider constructive criticism, lack of testing (discussed later), and other defensive patterns fit into this particular trap. This trap is sometimes sprung by time pressures.

Remedies: Check and recheck the logic of the proposed solutions. Try constructing the chain in reverse, i.e., stating the proposition in reverse order. If the (solution) *had* been in place, the *event or problem* probably would not have occurred because the *cause* would have been eliminated or mitigated (or something like this, depending upon the situation).

Although the rules of formal logic are fairly technical, the proposed solution(s) also can be evaluated by this simple test: Does the stated conclusion reasonably follow from the stated premises? Does the proposed solution reasonably line up with the original problem and its cause? For example, if revising procedures is proffered as the solution to a particular event and failure to follow procedures was one of the conditions noted, then revising procedures would not seem to line up. See Figure 5.1 for visualization of this concept.

A practical way to visualize this lineup is to construct a solutions matrix. As the analysis proceeds, the problem, assigned cause, and proposed solution may be entered into a form such as that shown in Table 5.1. In addition to observing the lineup of the items, this matrix can be

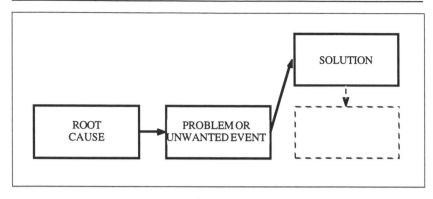

Figure 5.1
"Lining Up" the Solution

useful in the subsequent evaluation of proposed solutions as well as identifying specific fixes that might be required and those that are repetitive and may therefore be combined.

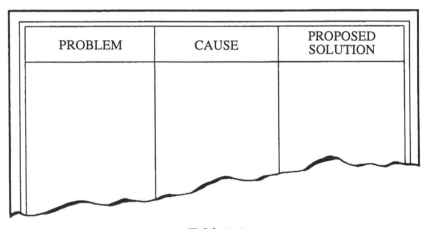

Table 5.1
Solutions Matrix

Other columns may be added by users if desired. For example, it may be useful to add columns for features and attributes that will be used in the evaluation stage (e.g., cost, probability of occurrence or success). The reader is referred to Chapter 6 for further discussion of this subject.

Devising Solutions

The previous section pointed out some of the traps to avoid when devising potential solutions. The following describes the development of solutions using the scientific approach.

Defining the Problem

The first logical step in devising solutions should be to recheck the definition of the problem as well as the root cause analysis.

Re-examine the reported problem. The logical starting point is the particular problem description or report which initiated the sequence; however, experience suggests that this information should only be considered as preliminary. Considerable bias may be present, the data may be far from complete, the reporting mechanism itself may have influenced the statement, etc. Those who examine reported problems on a continual basis can attest to how different the problem can be from the words provided on the initial description.

When reviewing the problem, it is important to clearly understand exactly what is being represented. Was it a single occurrence? Could it be considered random on prima facie evidence, or was it just a single instance of a recurring problem? If it was a single occurrence, what suggests the event can be considered as isolated? Was this event in some way connected to another, whether suggested in the problem report or not?

These and similar questions must be addressed when reviewing the problem. Shortcuts taken here will effectively limit the choice of an effective solution and thereby seriously affect the overall effort.

The root cause analysis conducted also should be reviewed. Given adequate problem description through the gathering of the appropriate data, it is worthwhile to go over the analysis to ensure that the process was properly performed and that adequate provisions were made regarding the evidence. The final result should be considered a reasonable problem and cause relationship.

One common error in root cause analyses is that they are less than complete. In going through the analysis, there is a tendency to find the *first* plausible cause for a problem or fault and then to terminate the analysis. Other possible reasons are either ignored or given short shrift. Careful review of the completed analysis may disclose this error in the analysis process.

Formulating Hypotheses

After the review of the problem and root cause analysis is completed, the next step is to devise a number of possible solutions. Once again, this set of solutions ideally represents not only the most obvious, but those that are novel or imaginative. The next question must be: How many solutions are appropriate?

There is no clear answer to this question. A good example is the story of Thomas Edison, who unsuccessfully tried over 1,200 different materials for an electric lightbulb filament. Chided for failing that many times, Edison simply replied, "I have discovered 1,200 materials that don't work." He then proceeded to find one that *did* work.

Obviously, the number of appropriate solutions is influenced by the nature of the particular problem and cause, programmatic considerations, time and cost constraints, and other factors. At this stage of the process, however, it is better to list all possible solutions (as in brainstorming); the subsequent evaluation stage will effectively sort these solutions. Remember that one of the primary rules of brainstorming is not to constrain the flow of ideas; at this point, any attempt at evaluating or otherwise sorting the ideas during the process should not be allowed.

Decision theory texts are quite clear as to the proper number of potential solutions. If a decision diagram to represent a decision with all of its possible outcomes is to be properly constructed, *all* possible choices must be included. Although it is virtually impossible to list all possible solutions (disregarding the time it would take to do so), the developed list of potential solutions should be as complete as possible.

This is a good time to ask others: "What else might be done?" Often this approach will result in a number of new ideas. Get other disciplines involved. The problem might not be within their normal purview, but their outlooks and differing opinions may be refreshing as well as valuable and help formulate solutions that might have otherwise been overlooked.

Gathering Appropriate Data

Gathering appropriate data, the next step in the scientific method, will also be discussed in Chapter 6, since it pertains to the evaluation and problem solving stages. The gathering of appropriate data is vital to the formulation of a set of potential solutions. Quite often when developing solutions, it is helpful to cast a glance sideways at potential fixes. Some of the more interesting solutions to problems often come from areas or disciplines outside of one's immediate area of expertise. An excellent example of this is the influx of novel concepts in public education that are being transferred from private sector training practices, which in turn were borrowed from the military (public sector).

Develop a wider view of problems and avoid unnecessary restrictions. If it appears *even* remotely possible that a particular solution *might* work, explore that option to the extent necessary to frame the proposed solution. Any art teacher will advise that sometimes all that is needed is a different perspective to make an otherwise dull picture interesting and meaningful. Realizing that the problem (and potential solution) can be viewed differently is an important consideration.

Gathering additional data, along with testing the solutions and developing the final conclusion, will be covered in further detail in Chapter 6.

Types of Solutions

When developing solutions, it is helpful to consider the solutions to be either long vs. short term and targeted vs. generic. The distinction is important in framing the solution (described below), as well as in considering whether or not all options have been explored.

Long vs. Short Term
The time frame and expected results of implementing proposed solutions are important aspects to consider. For example, personnel training often is listed as a potential fix for a problem. Indeed it might be a solution, except that the effects of training tend to wear off. This makes its value as a long-term solution suspect. If the needed training is not implemented on a continual basis, the problem of personnel turnover and replacement will negatively impact this solution. Conversely, if the training is to be repeated, will the training program design include refresher sessions (with needed updates) after the initial training is conducted? In other words, "provide the necessary training" is only a partial solution. The short- and long-term aspects must also be addressed as part of the solution for it to be considered complete.

Targeted vs. Generic
The solution provided should be examined in terms of its *specificity*. Is the proposed fix targeted and specific to the problem at hand, or does it represent a broader, more generic solution? This does not suggest targeted approaches are necessarily inadequate, but that the intended scope of the proposed solution should be understood and clearly stated.

Using the same example (training), it is important to examine whether the proposed training is specifically targeted toward the problem or intended to include the problem with larger, more generic issues that might be involved. For example, you might want to provide toolbox or on the job training for craftsmen on the proper way to lock out and tag equipment that has been removed from service for maintenance or repair. This represents a targeted approach to a fairly specific problem. If on the other hand you want to use a more generic approach, you might include this specific topic with others as part of overall training on the subject of safety. This latter approach might be considered more proactive in those cases where the surfaced problem is considered indicative of a general lack of understanding regarding safety issues or less-than-adequate work practices on the part of maintenance personnel. If the problem is determined to be more or less random or particular information that was missed (not supplied), or new practice, then the targeted approach, training on the specific issue of locking out and tagging equipment, is far more appropriate. In fact, it might be considered wasteful to overreact by putting into place a more elaborate training program than necessary.

Some Techniques
The process of devising solutions has been discussed in conceptual terms throughout this chapter. We will now provide some advice to aid problem solvers in developing a list of potential solutions.

Reduce Solution to Its Most Basic Form: Quite often the solution, as stated, is limiting. It represents only one solution within a larger set of possible answers. For example, "putting on socks and shoes" could be considered a partial solution within the broader statement "cover your feet" or "provide foot protection." There are many other ways to provide foot protection than just socks and shoes. By looking at the proposed solution in its more basic or generic form, other means of covering or protecting your feet might come to mind. Look at form, fit, and function; other answers may provide equally effective results.

Write Down All Obvious Solutions First: Before developing any particular solution further, make sure the list of obvious solutions is as complete as possible. Once you get into the detail, you may forget to double back and check this. This results in potential solutions being overlooked. Get all obvious solutions down as soon as possible. Also, by looking over this list you may think of other solutions (see below).

Write Down Any Other Ideas That Come Up: Once again, before proceeding to detail your ideas, write down any other potential solutions which might occur to you. Add any "might work" solutions; further development may eliminate them, but don't make that decision yet. Do a little freewheeling in your thinking.

Replace Factors to See If New Solution Emerges: Sometimes removing one or more of the factors that must be considered as part of the solution will aid in seeing entirely new alternatives. In fact, you may discover that they were not really factors in the first place. For example, suppose Edison had started with the premise that he wished to develop a better candle.

Branching Suggests More Alternatives: Draw a simple diagram like that shown in Figure 5.2. It will help you to consider the alternatives. Continue branching as long as you can; new possibilities can emerge in this fashion. Let's consider the simple situation of discovering a flat tire on your automobile. The most obvious answer is to replace the tire with the spare. However, by drawing the diagram shown, it can be seen that there are any number of alternatives that could be considered, depending upon the situation. Based upon the situation, one alternative may be better.

Consider Any Constraints: This might sound like heresy, but the purpose of considering constraints can be used prospectively to suggest additional solutions. Consider the earlier example of putting on socks and shoes. Assuming previous advice of reducing the solution need statement

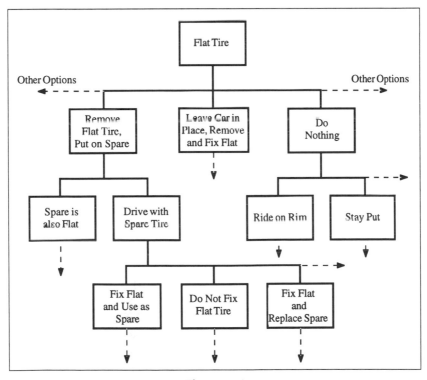

Figure 5.2
Alternate Solutions Diagram

to a more basic form has been taken, the problem has been reduced to covering one's feet. The addition of deep snow (a constraint on the solution that must be considered) may suggest that normal street shoes, sneakers, or another approach may not be appropriate. The constraint has suggested snowshoes or some solution that will effectively distribute the person's weight to avoid sinking in the deep snow. Based on all of the advice given so far, however, the constraint should not suggest snowshoes, but rather a means to avoid sinking into the deep snow. Right?

Once a set of solutions has been derived, the next step is to make sure they are adequately described in order to allow others to understand and evaluate them.

Preparing Solutions

This section discusses two items: framing the potential solutions and providing additional information/criteria which may be needed during the evaluation phase. Information that will be useful during the evaluation of proposed solutions includes the following:

■ Clear statement and identification of the essential features of each proposed solution
■ Provision of the attributes of the proposed solution
■ Qualitative or quantitative measures that may be used during their evaluation

Determining the Essential Features

It is important to capture the *essence* of the proposed solution. Terms such as *goals* or *objectives* can be applied here. The solution should be described, in summary form, in terms of its essential features. If several *options* are included within a particular proposed solution, they should be clearly indicated, with or without any preference attached.

Determining the essential features of proposed solutions is necessary not only for the subsequent evaluation phase, but for eventual presentation of solutions to management. The process of stating a proposed solution in terms of its essential features will sometimes also disclose omissions or the need for possible redirection. Consider this operation as the final polish; it may reveal defects that a little added refinement (repolishing) can easily remove.

Providing the Attributes

The attributes of a proposed solution are very much like attributes used in item or equipment inspection. Attributes are characteristics or properties that may be observed or measured. By verification, comparison, or grading of these attributes, a decision (usually regarding the acceptability of the item) can be made. In the case of proposed solutions, similar attributes aid subsequent evaluator(s) in making a choice between alternatives.

This step consists of linking the psychological concepts of objectives, goals, and essential features to objective measures that will be used during the subsequent evaluation phase. This is accomplished by describing the attributes (e.g., specific characteristics or properties). These attributes may also be used later to evaluate the effectiveness of an implemented solution.

It is important to recognize that certain attributes may be stated in extra-organizational terms. As an example, consider the technical training provided by the armed forces. This training is necessary based on the increased complexity of weapons systems (direct need), but has also produced a supply of technically competent individuals in the subsequent civilian job market (subsequent benefit). The magnitude of the required training effort by the armed forces is obviously influenced by high (and vocational) school curricula. This is recognized and demonstrated by the armed forces' admonition to "stay in school" prior to entry into the service. On the other hand, in many cases the training provided has lessened the required training by private industry. These are (and should be) included as relevant attributes by the armed forces in their recruitment efforts.

Developing Qualitative and Quantitative Measures

A quantitative measure can be represented by a scale, measurement, or range of values that may be used to describe the relative level of an attribute. To be useful, this measure should be highly correlated to the attribute, much as test results should indicate the level of knowledge of a subject. Test validity remains a continuing concern to most educators.

In certain situations, it is sometimes difficult to assign quantitative measures to proposed solutions. Solutions may only be described in terms of qualitative terms. Certain social programs are an excellent example, i.e., what criteria should be applied to measure the effects of childcare support?

Certain solutions can be measured only in terms of risk avoidance or mitigation. This is especially true for events yet to happen and, therefore, can only be probabilistically estimated in terms of their occurrence or postulated events for which the consequences are altogether unacceptable.

Trying Out the Solutions

It is good practice to review potential solutions with the affected organizations. At first this might sound heretical or like an attempt to assuage potential dissatisfactions, but it is intended as practical advice. The organization(s) responsible for corrective, preventive, or adaptive actions might provide valuable input to solutions that have been framed or suggest others that have not yet been considered. Eventually they will have to buy into the solution and in being part of the process develop a sense of ownership.

There may be constraints to a proposed solution that the organization may be able to identify. This is not to suggest a watering down process, but one that hopefully will make the proposed solution more viable. On this subject, however, analysts should be reminded that, in the real world, a less-than-perfect solution is better than none at all or one that will not be implemented because it is too elaborate. This is one more example of the art being as important as the science.

A Closing Story

No discussion of developing proposed solutions would be complete without the well-known (and true) story of the trailer truck wedged under a bridge. The driver had either ignored or missed the usual sign advising the height of an upcoming underpass. The momentum of the vehicle caused the semi-trailer to become firmly wedged under the bridge.

Traffic was backed up for miles. The driver, police, state engineers, and a host of other involved personnel were considering a number of possible actions. None of these were particularly inventive; some were just plain destructive (such as cutting apart the trailer). No one had yet developed a clearly attractive solution.

Then a little boy who had been watching intently asked, "Why don't you let some air out of the tires?" They did this and it worked.

Summary

We have examined the process of devising solutions to a problem, including looking at the root cause(s) of the problem. The next chapter will discuss how these proposed solutions may be evaluated. Aside from the mechanisms involved in the thought processes utilized, cautions regarding faulty or clouded thinking, and some guidance regarding the proper approach to developing solutions, the following points should be remembered:

Number of Solutions

Proposed solutions provided for each problem should be as many and as varied as possible, ranging from the most obvious to those that are imaginative and creative. The "right" number of solutions is *all* of those that *might* correct the problem.

Types of Solutions

Proposed solutions should be considered for both their short- and long-term effects. Solutions also should be identified as to whether they are targeted to the specific situation or are more generic in nature.

Framing of Solutions

Proposed solutions should include a summary of their essential features and provide attributes which can be used during their evaluation.

6

EVALUATING SOLUTIONS

"The prologues are over. ... It is time to choose."

—Wallace Stevens (1879-1955),
Asides on the Oboe, 1942

Introduction

Referring again to Webster, the word "evaluation" is defined as "to determine the worth of; to find the amount or value of; to appraise." The words "worth," "value," and "appraise" all aptly describe the evaluation process discussed in this chapter.

The process of evaluating proposed solutions to a particular problem is straightforward when conducted properly. Each of the proposed solutions (whose development was discussed in Chapter 5) should be first appraised in terms of validity and completeness, then assigned some measure of relative value or worth. This relative value can then be used as criteria for evaluation and the eventual selection of the best solution. The evaluation process, to be totally effective, must also consider any constraints which may be imposed by the system itself.

The evaluation process could be considered one of reduction, of weighing alternatives, applying criteria or choice factors, following some rules or pattern of logic, until only one solution remains. This evaluation process, however, should be more than an unformatted assessment, random selection, or personal choice. The process is all the more intriguing because it involves value and preference systems, which are often uncovered during the evaluation process.

The evaluation process is every bit as important as the other activities discussed so far: accurate problem definition, effective root cause analysis, and the development of appropriate solutions. All the best work up front can easily be compromised by an improper or biased evaluation. This chapter will examine the evaluation process with the intent of providing sufficient explanation to help the reader understand its mechanics.

The Evaluation Process

The investigation of the process of evaluating proposed solutions to an event or problem will focus on the following topics:

- Initial steps in evaluating solutions
- Testing solutions
- The concept of barriers
- Recognizing constraints
- The value of perfect information
- Quantifying personal preference values
- Recognizing invalid solutions

Initial Steps in Evaluating Solutions

Unless some method of scoring is provided in the selection process, all proposed solutions may appear equally attractive or suitable. In some situations, the scoring system may already be specified. Predetermined weighting factors may be designated for portions (or all) of the potential solutions. An example of this might be the scoring system used to rank candidates for a particular job opening in the government sector. A certain number of points are assigned for years of experience, veteran's status, etc., with the composite final score computed for each of the candidates. It is essentially this score that is used to select the successful job applicant.

An effective ranking system will utilize some form of evaluation units; usually scalar values. These units might be implementation costs (dollars or man-hours) associated with the particular solution (although evaluating solutions only on cost could be disastrous), expected payoff periods (the same caution is advised), a cost-benefit analysis (better), etc. The ranking system might also be based upon (or include) less quantifiable factors such as:

- The number and/or type of potential problems that may be encountered during implementation
- System constraints
- How difficult the solution will be to implement
- Probability of success, etc.

There is no standard or preferred evaluation unit that can be universally applied. In fact, it could be argued that there are so many factors involved and that the nature of the problem itself and the organizational factors dictate the criteria to be applied. The only commonality might be that, regardless of the criteria used, any evaluation should proceed in some systematic fashion.

If evaluation units were assigned each proposed solution during the developmental phase, the evaluation process should be fairly straightforward. However, if evaluation units are not provided with the proposed solution, they will need to be developed as part of the evaluation process. As already suggested, the choice of evaluation units to apply will depend on the particular problem, its cause, and the risk or hazard factors, as well as organizational values and attitudes. For example, cost of implementation for safety-related or other high-risk-problem solutions becomes a legitimate consideration only for those solutions which correct the dangerous conditions. All those proposed solutions which do not correct the situation need not be considered further. Cost becomes a secondary or lower level criteria.

Although the cost factor (of itself) may not be suitable for evaluating certain solutions, there are a number of situations in which it may be. Consider the family decision of buying a new car or home. Regardless of its appeal, the choice between alternatives might eventually be based on the simple cost criterion: "We just can't afford it." This sole measure might be reason enough and entirely appropriate provided there are no other intervening factors.

Obviously it is helpful to first weed out any solutions that are manifestly invalid. Invalid solutions are those that are not effective in terms of all or some of the previously mentioned criteria. Invalid solutions also include those that cannot be effectively implemented or are incomplete (rendering them unusable in their present format).

It is not always easy to recognize an invalid solution. Many solutions are borderline. For example, revising written procedures is a favorite fix for all kinds of problems. However, if personnel don't refer to and use these procedures as part of their routine activities, simply revising these procedures represents a partial (incomplete) solution. A more complete solution dictates that personnel be properly trained in these revised procedures and ensures that they use these procedures in the future. The truly complete fix also requires monitoring the situation to ensure they do use the proper procedure(s). Thus, in most cases the solution of revising procedures requires further definition before evaluation can proceed. At this point, the solution can be discarded, revised, strengthened, or put aside to save for future reconsideration. Further discussion on recognizing invalid solutions is provided later in this chapter.

Testing Solutions

An important step in evaluating solutions is to ask, "Will the proposed solution correct the problem?" It would seem indisputable that the subject solution, by the very fact it was proposed, was *intended* to solve the problem, but it may not. In a few instances, the proposed solution may not only be ineffective but could worsen the situation. The author is reminded of some of the patent cough medicines of his childhood that not only did not seem to lessen the coughing but introduced nausea as a further misery.

One of the easiest ways to test solutions is to apply simple mathematical logic. Consider the following equation:

Root cause + proposed solution = no further occurrences

By formatting the proposed solution in this manner, the effectiveness of the solution may be concluded. Another test might be to state the problem or event, its root cause, and the proposed solution in the following sentence: "The [proposed solution] should correct [the root cause] which caused [the problem or event]." Say it out loud and see if it sounds right. Does it ring true or does it sound shaky? Use no other criteria during this process than the inherent logic of the chained statement. Get other opinions.

The processes described above can also be thought of as a process of lining up. The solution should proceed from the root cause and the problem in a straightforward, logical manner. It should be obvious. It should make sense. Refer again to Figure 5.1 for a graphic depiction of this concept.

Testing As a Barrier

Considering the proposed solution as a potential barrier to fault or problem recurrence is another evaluation technique that can be used. A barrier is defined as something that should prevent an event from occurring or an unwanted condition from existing. Barriers are discussed in considerable detail in Chapter 9. For the purpose of this discussion, however, it is only necessary to understand that a barrier is a preventive measure.

The process is rather direct. Think of the proposed solution in terms of whether or not it will create an effective barrier. This is a practical way to test the solution's effectiveness. Will the solution correct the problem? Will it prevent the problem's recurrence? Does the solution strengthen an existing barrier or make a failed barrier more effective? If it is a new barrier, will it effectively resolve the current situation? What else will be required to make the solution work?

Barriers also can be tested prospectively. Security personnel do this routinely. How can the barrier be circumvented or breached? Postulate ways or situations as to how the barrier might fail, or its intended purpose be defeated. If the barrier is going to fail, it is better to find out now than wait until after the solution has already been implemented. At this point there is probably time to make any needed adjustments. Better now than later, when the breakdown of the barrier could cause serious problems.

Recognizing Constraints

Proposed solutions also should be evaluated in terms of any conditions that may restrict or constrain their effectiveness or ability to be implemented. These constraints may either be embedded within the solution itself or imposed by system factors, such as resource requirements and others.

Consider again the previous example of personnel training as a proposed solution. Constraints that might be considered as part of this solution's evaluation might include the following:

- Will the needed training be adequately defined and effectively implemented?
- Are the needed instructors available?
- Will schedules be established and the personnel needing training be made available?
- Will measures be provided to assess training performances?

Each proposed solution should be evaluated for any constraints. In essence, is each proposed solution "doable"? Many proposals are unrealistic, not necessarily in concept, but in terms of their ability to be successfully implemented. Not considering constraints will affect the eventual outcome of installed corrections unless adequate provision for these obstacles is first considered.

The Value of Perfect Information

Decision theory provides an interesting concept: having perfect information. Perfect information means that all the facts and all the potential difficulties or consequences of a decision are known prior to its being made. There is no uncertainty involved.

In real life, there always will be some uncertainty involved in every decision. By definition, if the decision was made on the basis of perfect information, it will always be correct. However, the cost of obtaining better (even if imperfect) information can be higher than the consequences of a wrong choice. Additionally, the time required to obtain this added information might be unreasonable. This delay could hinder decisions from being made in a timely fashion.

Perfect information should not be a prerequisite to the evaluation of proposed solutions; however, the analyst should generally attempt to get as close to this goal as practical by gathering all available information to allow as valid and complete an assessment as possible. The important lesson here is that the analyst learn to recognize the potential uncertainty in any information provided and attempt to provide some form of countermeasure to offset potential uncertainties.

Quantifying Personal Preference Values

When evaluating solutions, it is important to recognize that personal and organizational bias may enter in, whether consciously or not. This will result in certain proposed solutions receiving higher scores, simply due to this preference.

There are techniques in decision theory that can be used to isolate and quantify these preference values. It is not the intention to explore these in this book, but analysts who perform evaluations on a continual basis may wish to consult with decision theory texts to further understand these techniques and thereby help them effectively weigh proposed solutions. Personal or organizational preferences certainly play a big role in the evaluation process. For example, when a company introduces a new product, production personnel might provide a completely different perspective than marketing and sales personnel. One evaluator will see the product in terms of new opportunities or needed additions, and the other simply as a new set of problems. It is not suggested that this bias is necessarily invalid, just that it be recognized. Like the previously discussed recognition that information may be imperfect or imprecise, compensation for any discovered bias may also be required.

Recognizing Invalid Solutions

Quite simply, invalid solutions are those that won't work. Solutions may not work for a number of reasons, such as embedded flaws, failure to consider implementation requirements, lack of understanding of the system, commitment of management, or other constraints.

The evaluator must learn to recognize invalid and marginal solutions. Invalid solutions clearly will not work; however, many solutions are marginal and may have some possibility for success. This is where a classification process is needed. Although solutions that won't work should be set aside, other solutions need to be further developed or improved before the evaluation process can continue.

Methods of Evaluation

The following are methods that may be used either individually or in combination to evaluate potential solutions. The technique(s) chosen will depend on a number of factors, including the specific problem and root cause, as well as organizational values and attitudes.

Cost, Compliance, and Other Factors

The simplest evaluations are those which can be made based upon specific, well-defined, and/or easily quantified factors, such as cost or compliance with predetermined requirements. For example, in the case of compliance with most standards, the evaluation already has a built-in acceptability threshold. All proposed solutions that do not guarantee compliance can automatically be declared invalid. When codes, standards, regulations, or other fairly defined criteria must be met, the evaluation process is simpler. Only those solutions which meet the minimum requirements must be evaluated further.

An evaluation using cost criteria also is relatively straightforward. Considering cost alone, however, can often lead to false conclusions; the *value* of the solution should be considered. Value may or may not be directly related to cost. The concept of value is familiar to most consumers and will be examined in further detail in the section "Cost-Benefit and Risk-Benefit."

Constructability Review

This concept is familiar to those with either a manufacturing or construction background. The proposal is evaluated in terms of feasibility. Implementation, manufacturing, or constructability problems are noted during the review. A constructability review almost always involves more than one discipline. The review usually involves those who will be responsible for the proposed solution and its implementation. For example, if training is the proposed fix, the proposed solution should be jointly reviewed by the personnel responsible for conducting the training, as well as the cognizant management from those areas targeted to receive the training.

Properly conducted, a constructability review is a hard review conducted by the potential implementors themselves. All aspects of the solutions need to be considered in order that a detailed plan to implement the solution can be developed. Any expected problems should be noted, preliminary resource allocations and schedules provided, and further information that may be necessary identified.

Cost-Benefit and Risk-Benefit

Cost-benefit analyses are presented in many management or economics texts. When the benefit can be expressed in terms of dollars, each proposed solution can be measured in terms of return on investment. For example, if training will result in increased production, it is simple to calculate the return. If training will result in fewer downtime hours, it can be compared easily in terms of the same common denominator: dollars. The same is true for decreased absenteeism, increased employee retention, etc.

There are, however, real, substantial benefits which cannot be expressed in dollars. Many of these fall into the category of corporate goodwill or social responsibility, (e.g., child support and elderly care). The comparison and grading of such benefits must be made on a different basis, using an aesthetic or other measurement scale, such as intrinsic value.

In other situations, solutions cannot be specifically evaluated against any expected benefit, but are designed to mitigate or eliminate a real or potential risk. Safety problems often are of this nature. When performing a risk-benefit evaluation, the avoidance aspect rating is a significant consideration: the lower the potential for exposure to risk, the higher the rating. The thinking for this type of analysis is somewhat reversed from that of a cost-benefit analysis.

It is important to interject a caution here. It is almost impossible to reduce risk to zero. The cost would be prohibitive. We live with a certain amount of risk and consider it acceptable in most cases. Consider the example of airport security. The threat of firearms or explosives being brought on board airline flights could be substantially reduced by performing full body searches, emptying all luggage, searching through all packages loaded as baggage, etc. However, passengers would have to arrive for their flight several hours in advance if such drastic security measures were implemented. Although the risk would be substantially reduced, the cost of such an effort would not be worth its benefit under normal circumstances. However, if terrorism was a real possibility, risk management might suggest any or all of these measures as not only appropriate but necessary and prudent.

Qualitative vs. Quantitative

Evaluation units expressed in quantitative terms, especially if they are expressed in the same terms as the solution cost (e.g., dollars, hours), provide the easiest means to evaluate proposed solutions. Quantitative measures, however, cannot always be applied to the evaluation of proposed solutions. Rather than abandon the concepts discussed thus far, these measures need to be converted to some type of scale, even if aesthetic, to enable the solutions to be ranked.

The analyst continually faces the problem of having to decide which evaluation measures to apply. Often, both quantitative and qualitative criteria will be applied to the same proposed solution. If this is done, there must be thought given as to how these different measures will be combined. How will these evaluation measures be used in determining the final score? Will a quantitative measure always be considered more important than any qualitative measure, or will they be considered equal? It also should be pointed out that the mix will be different for various organizations, the circumstances and timing, the magnitude of the problem and its probable impact, etc. There is no hard and fast general rule that can be applied.

Time Frame

Solutions may be evaluated in terms of how soon the benefits or their expected results will be realized. Solutions that provide the quickest results will generally be given the highest score. This is, however, only true when the solutions being compared have the same cost and chance of success. The evaluation criteria might not only include the time to implement or the time to expected results, but also their lasting power.

When considering preventive measures, it is easy to make this term synonymous with long-term or lasting results. The two are different concepts. Strictly speaking, preventive measures are intended to eliminate the event or problem. Corrective measures are primarily directed at solving the problem at hand.

Examination of both aspects (expected duration vs. corrective/preventive content) of any proposed solution can provide valuable insight. Each proposed solution is first given a rating on a scale of 1 to 10 (or any other value desired) in terms of short- vs. long-term effect or staying power. Then the same solution can be given a score of 1 to 10 in terms of its primary intent: correcting the immediate problem vs. preventing a similar problem in the future.

The results of each set of scores may then be plotted as shown in Figure 6.1. Point A represents a short-term corrective action (1,1); Point B a long-term preventive action (10,10); Point C a long-term corrective action (1,10), etc.

At first glance it might appear that a 10,10 score is best. This may not be true. This score implies that the action deals only with prevention (by definition), thereby ignoring correction of the problem at hand.

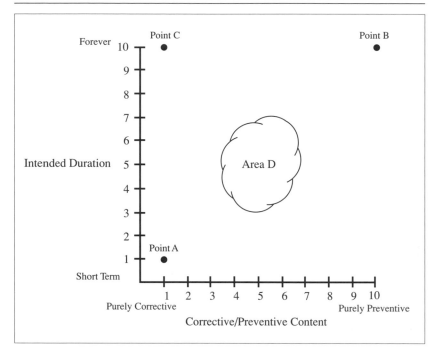

Figure 6.1
Evaluation Matrix

Also, the score implies a long-term action. It may not be desirable to leave this in place indefinitely. For example, a bank experiencing problems in the daily tallies may institute 100 percent verification by the head teller of all calculations. This may prevent future problems but could introduce considerable delays and overhead expense if continued indefinitely.

It also is true that a score of 1,1 may be the most appropriate solution for a problem. If an event or problem is peculiar or unique, it probably makes little sense but to fix it and move on.

A score of 1,10 (long-term corrective action) could likewise be the best solution for another type of event or situation. Consider the case of a light bulb burning out. Routine replacement of the bulb when it burns out would generally receive a 1,10 score using the above numbering system. Routinely correcting the problem as it occurs in a predetermined manner may be the most logical and prudent solution.

What emerges, of course, is that there is no perfect value. Depending upon the particular problem, the rating of the best solution can be quite different. It is likely, however, that for *most* problems, the solution scores will fall somewhere in the region shown as D in Figure 6.1.

Appropriate attention will be paid to fixing the immediate problem, as well as preventing its recurrence, and there will be an intended duration for the measure to be in effect, somewhere between a few days or weeks and forever.

Probability Assessments

Another technique that may be used to evaluate proposed solutions is its probability of success. Each proposed solution can be assessed by assigning probabilities to its chance of success or failure. This aids in the sorting process, since those with a low probability of success usually can be disregarded. Even if the assigned probability of success or failure is somewhat subjective, the picture will be clearer than if each proposed solution is given an equal chance for success (which is the case when no probabilities are assigned). In fact, logic dictates that an equal chance of success for all alternatives is not realistic, unless you are flipping a coin.

Probabilities may be assigned based on previous experience or similar situations. Probabilities also can be assigned on a subjective basis, formulated on knowledge of current operations, or through other criteria.

These assigned probabilities could be multiplied by any quantitative evaluation unit assigned to each proposed solution to obtain expected values. As an example of expected value, a lottery ticket could be said to represent millions of dollars (results). The chance of achieving this result, however, also needs to be considered. The odds of actually winning the lottery must be multiplied by that dollar amount, yielding an expected value for the ticket. If you paid $1 for a lottery ticket for which there was a $1 million jackpot and you had a one in a million chance of winning, then the expected value of your ticket is exactly what you paid for it.

Closing Story

No doubt, everyone is familiar with the story of the emperor's new clothes. No one dared tell him that he was, in fact, quite naked. The story ends with a child, perhaps not knowing better nor recognizing the possible consequences of his actions, telling the emperor the truth.

Assuming you are a courtier and the child's remarks had not yet been voiced, what potential actions to apprise the emperor might you consider? Using some of the criteria provided in this chapter, evaluate these approaches, including their probable success (or cost).

Summary

This chapter has discussed a number of techniques that may be utilized to evaluate potential solutions developed as a result of root cause analysis. The exact evaluation technique used will be influenced by several factors, which include the nature of the problem itself, its root cause, the basic types of proposed solutions, and organizational values and attitudes. It is important that the solution be tried for fit against these criteria and that any constraints or limitations be identified.

Quantitative evaluation criteria are perhaps the easiest to use, but there are many situations in which they cannot be applied. In those cases, some values must be assigned to the qualitative aspects of each solution to help put them in some sort of order.

Factors, such as the time required to implement these solutions, may be used. However, the expected duration of the proposed solution as well as its mix of corrective and preventive action content also must be considered. Adding probabilities of success or failure can aid in the evaluation and may provide a clearer picture of expected results. Remember that the most important question will always be, "Will the proposed solution effectively correct and prevent recurrence of the problem?"

7

SYSTEM CONSIDERATIONS

"It really does matter whether you win or lose and this definitely depends on how you play the game."

—Modified quote by the authors, 1991

Introduction

It must be apparent by now that an effective root cause analysis system involves more than the application of the analysis techniques described in this book. In earlier chapters, the definition of the problem, gathering of appropriate information, development of potential solutions, and subsequent evaluation of these solutions were discussed. What is eventually done with the final solution is equally important. Otherwise, the overall root cause analysis effort is poorly implemented.

This chapter describes some actions that may be taken by management to measure the effectiveness of installed root cause analysis systems. The focus of this assessment will properly be on this system's output. It is the solution of problems and unwanted events, as well as the prevention of similar situations in the future, that will ultimately determine the real effectiveness of any installed root cause analysis system.

Facing the Facts

One of the most prevalent reasons root cause analysis systems do not work is simply that the results are not utilized or applied. Root cause analysis techniques identify the real reason that problems or unwanted conditions occur. Properly done, considerable effort has already been expended in gathering pertinent information, analyzing the problem, devising potential solutions, and then selecting the most appropriate solution. What is wrong is not what was done, but the answer itself. Nobody likes it.

For example, it is reasonable to expect that a fair proportion of surfaced problems will be caused by less-than-adequate management methods. Although the percentage may differ from one organization to another, generally it is the predominant root cause. Since the analysis results are given to management, this is unwelcome news. After all, management is supposed to solve problems, not create them.

A certain amount of bias and predisposition toward solutions is to be expected. There may be traditional or accepted reasons for problems that have to be set aside. There may even be suggestions as to how the analysis may be improved. Although there may be perspectives that are unknown to the analyst, changes or alterations should not be allowed to introduce bias to the point that whatever effort has been spent on seeking the truth is wasted. The advice here is simple: Having done all you should do, *face the facts* even if you don't like or agree with them.

This obvious and straightforward advice might seem unnecessary, but it has already been pointed out that disregarding the results is the reason most root cause efforts fail. They fail in practice, not principle.

Failure to act on identified causes of problems is even worse than not recognizing them in the first place. Considerable effort and monies will have been expended for no worthwhile purpose. If an organization is not prepared to *walk the talk*, then it should avoid putting in place something that will only be disregarded or alibied away. It has been mentioned that TQM is based on continual improvement. Recognition of these identified opportunities for improvement is a necessary ingredient for successful implementation of an effective root cause analysis system.

Measuring the Effectiveness of Root Cause Analysis

The most often asked question is "How can I measure the effectiveness of root cause analysis efforts?" This chapter explores some of these measures, but the underlying basis for the answer is quite simple: Are we finding, identifying, fixing, and preventing problems or, more simply, are we doing better?

This is not simply a numbers game. The total number of faults or problems before and after root cause analysis efforts were initiated would seem an easy measure. But an assessment based solely on the frequency of problems or unwanted events is, at best, cursory. The number of reported problems can be influenced by changing the reporting system or applying different criteria. In addition, effective root cause analysis may point out problems that were not recognized as such before. It has effected a greater sensitivity to embedded faults in the system, which should be viewed positively.

Root cause analysis also may point out a number of other potential problems, so the total number might now include these as well. We have already pointed out that this early identification should be considered a benefit to the organization. Also, what may be more important than the number of faults is the type of faults. The evaluation of the effectiveness of an installed root cause analysis system may be more qualitative than quantitative. For example, if you are working on a complete overhaul of the procedural system rather than revising a large number of procedures found less than adequate, you are probably on the right track. In this example you are working on the basic cause rather than on the symptoms.

Some specific suggestions regarding initiatives that may help measure the effectiveness of installed root cause analysis systems follow.

Initial and Periodic Assessments of System(s)

Auditing guidelines usually suggest that any program, system, or project should be audited *at least once* during its duration or annually. The guidelines further point out that the initial system audit should be conducted as soon as possible.

Although we are not discussing a formal audit, these same guidelines make sense when discussing assessments of a system or program. In our case, the effectiveness of the root cause analysis system should be evaluated as soon as possible after implementation. Obvious checklist questions that need to be addressed include the following.

- Have the goals and objectives been identified clearly?
- Has management buy-in and support been obtained?
- Has the effort been described to all participants?
- In what fashion and how often will the results be evaluated?
- Are any required procedures in place?
- Were the right people assigned in terms of experience and background?

- Have the assigned analysts been properly trained in the techniques?
- Have appropriate reporting mechanisms been established?
- Has selection criteria for problem analysis been set?
- Have corrective and preventive action systems been checked?
- Is there any trend system in place?

This list can be expanded or modified for your particular organization, but it gives some idea of evaluation measures that can be applied.

It should be noted that the questions listed apply to the mechanics of a root cause analysis system and do not constitute a true performance assessment. Judging the actual performance of root cause analysis efforts requires the application of entirely different standards which are based on achievement. A performance assessment looks at substance, rather than form. It is more likely to involve relative values based on subject matter expertise or external considerations, such as client satisfaction. For example, consider that the installed root cause analysis system is judged effective by positive responses to *all* the questions listed above, yet the level of customer complaints does not appear to be reduced. Clearly, something is wrong. Although the system appears to be working well, it is not properly focused or targeted.

This concept is visually described in Figure 7.1, showing the "target" of customer satisfaction. Figure 7.1 (a) shows hits all over the target, indicating a fairly unfocused effort. Figure 7.1 (b) shows an improvement in the focus with reasonable grouping of hits, although still not accurate in

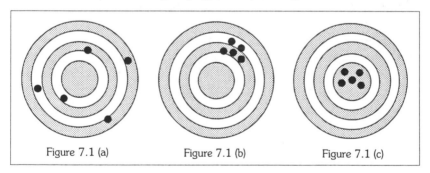

Figure 7.1 (a)   Figure 7.1 (b)   Figure 7.1 (c)

Figure 7.1
Effectiveness and Performance

terms of hitting the bullseye of customer satisfaction. This is analogous to a system that otherwise appears to work reasonably well but still fails to meet performance objectives. Figure 7.1 (c) illustrates the same basically effective system, but one that is now focused properly on its performance goal (customer satisfaction).

Implementation of Required Program Changes

There is a relatively straightforward means to determine the effectiveness of root cause analysis efforts. The focus of this evaluation should not be upon the elegance of the techniques utilized, nor the prescription provided the process, but upon the results. Are we recognizing and solving problems? Are we preventing their recurrence?

It follows then that an effective root cause analysis program, coupled with the necessary corrective/preventive action(s), should result in noticeable improvement in the process or activity. If the number and severity of surfaced problems or unwanted events has been drastically reduced, then the efforts may be judged successful. If even slight progress is seen in that direction, the effort could be considered potentially successful, with study made to discover hangups.

However, if either of these two positive indications are not noted, it is reasonable to assume that the efforts are not producing the intended results. What then? The answer is obvious. Change the system.

Concepts of Evolutionism vs. Creationism

There is a tendency to assume that everything must be right before any system is introduced, and to the extent that they can be, this is a good philosophy. Nothing is perfect, however, and delaying the implementation of systems such as problem reporting, problem analysis, and other similar mechanisms by which management can determine less than adequate situations makes no sense at all. Otherwise, once again management is playing blindman's bluff; they are unaware of potentially significant problems surrounding them.

The importance of planning in developing problem reporting, analysis, and solution systems cannot be overemphasized. The chances of success increase with the degree of system completeness. The adequacy of any system can be properly evaluated only during implementation. The effectiveness of any system still on the drawing board can only be estimated. Considering the current competitiveness situation, you *can* be blamed for not trying.

Most management textbooks also recommend the installation of short-term improvements, rather than to accumulate them or wait for the one big improvement. There is probably no large, truly effective system that was perfectly created. Deficiencies noted during the initial implementation or subsequent operation phases were translated into system changes that were required and made. Therefore, the process was one of evolution.

Two points emerge. The first point is that any system, when initially introduced, is likely to contain some embedded flaws. Accept this as plain fact and do not allow it to become the reason for delaying its implementation. The second point is that, as these expected flaws emerge, do not disregard them. Use them to fine tune the system.

Recognize that effective systems evolve and were not created that way. If for no other reason, changes will be needed as time and conditions change. The system itself might also force change by identifying less than adequate organizational, process, or activity conditions, and that's definitely OK. It's working.

Checking Results of Specific Actions
One of the important aspects of any effective root cause analysis/corrective/preventive action(s) system is the continual revisiting of installed action(s). This re-examination is important for two reasons. The first critical objective or reason is to determine the effectiveness of installed corrective/preventive actions in terms of reducing or eliminating the initial cause of the problem or unwanted condition. If this check is not performed, it is like an open loop system, since no feedback is provided as to how well the action (selected solution) is working. For any number of reasons, it may require modification. It may also be that one of the other (originally considered) solutions might have worked better, given the added perspective of seeing the implementation aspects. On the other hand, the corrective/preventive action may be working well. Checking the status and effectiveness of installed corrective or preventive actions not only makes sense, it should be considered a must.

The second reason for checking results is to determine if the correction is still needed. Quite often the surfaced problem and its cause have been remedied to the point that continued corrective or preventive action(s) is not required. Once this happens, the treatment is no longer needed and may be discontinued. You may also discover that some other, subsequent remedy has helped, so that the original treatment is now redundant. Or you may find that a series of previous corrections may be replaced by one which combines all the necessary features. Quite often, in implementing a series of corrective/preventive actions, it can be like putting Band-Aids™ over other Band-Aids.™ Checking now and then can help to identify if this is indeed the case.

There also is a dark side to this situation. Subsequent corrective or preventive action(s) can actually *reduce the effectiveness* of previous actions or, even more ominously, *make matters worse*. There is the curious logic here that two rights could make a wrong.

Some of the checklist questions introduced earlier that can be used in determining the results of specific corrective/preventive actions include the following:

- Were corrective actions properly installed or put into place?
- Have appropriate validation measures been included?
- Are periodic reviews for effectiveness, need for replacement, revision, or discontinuance conducted?
- Have modifications been made? Are they needed? Why?
- Have lessons learned been incorporated?

Managing Change

Recognizing that change may be necessary, it is important that any required change be managed properly. Further discussion of the need to understand, control, and predict the effects of change may be found in Chapter 8.

Revisions to installed corrective actions, as well as the system itself, may be needed as time passes or conditions change. Necessary modifications may also be suggested by the results themselves. Certain problems or conditions may require additional correction beyond those initially planned. Subsequent problems or conditions may have exacerbated previous faults or lessened the effect of installed corrective/preventive actions.

Bearing in mind that it is generally unwise to take medicine much beyond achieving a state of well-being, it is likewise advisable to consider revisiting some of these treatments. It may be necessary to tighten or open limits, adjust the previous baseline, or otherwise fine tune installed corrective/preventive actions.

In doing this, however, it is important to *treat any and all revisions as a new solution*. Only by subjecting each revision considered (however seemingly small) to the same rigor as that given the initial solution will there be sufficient assurance provided as to its correctness. This is basic quality assurance. The same philosophy used for design changes applies here.

Periodic Assessment of System

In like fashion, the overall system requires periodic assessment. Patterns may be discerned that are not detectable when examining individual corrective/preventive actions (fault corrections). Obviously, the main criteria for the systemwide assessment is: Are problems and unwanted conditions being identified and solved?

So far our focus has been on the problem reporting, root cause analysis, and fault correction portions of the system; however, it is worthwhile to re-examine the overall system. In the larger sense, all of this is not only part of, but should mesh with other portions of the TQM program. Figure 7.2 shows the aspects we have covered so far (solid lines) in the context of other elements of a TQM program.

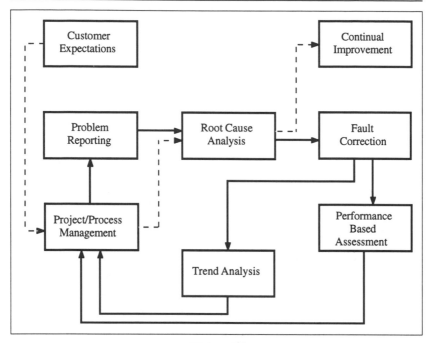

Figure 7.2
Overall System

The problem reporting, root cause analysis, and fault correction system ties back to project/process management through the mechanisms of an effective trend analysis and performance-based assessment system. Process/project management, as alluded to earlier, includes the necessary process and activity measurement and control features (e.g., determination of process/activity capability, statistical process control, and analysis of variance).

Another path shown is that of potential input to the root cause analysis and fault correction subsystem through defined customer/client expectations (dotted lines). This is portrayed to show that the same techniques may be utilized to examine shortfalls in expected performance. Dotted lines also illustrate the use of root cause analysis as the source for continual improvement activities. This concept of root cause analysis as a means of identifying the most obvious opportunities for improvement is presented throughout this book. Viewed as a mechanism which can be used in this fashion, the following questions may be asked:

1. Is the system effective in identifying and removing impediments to customer/client expectations?
2. Does the system result in (non-problem-related) opportunities for improvement?

The problem-related checklist questions therefore might include the following.

- Are all installed corrective and preventive actions effective?
- Is there the proper balance between these actions?
- Are there instances of overlapping corrective and preventive actions, or even duplications?
- Have measures been put in place to validate specific as well as overall results? Are they appropriate?
- Are mechanisms in place to revise or discontinue treatments that are duplicated, no longer required, or otherwise displaced?
- Have treatments been evaluated against their intended results?

Evaluating the further need for in-place measures and other constraints that may be unnecessary is every bit as important as installing them properly in the first place. It is easy to get into a corrective action spiral. It also is easy to fall into the trap of adding another layer of checks and balances to ensure that problems or unwanted conditions are minimized. You can spend as much or more time checking than doing. All of this is contrary to the basic TQM philosophy which stresses doing it right the first time.

Other non-problem-related questions which deal with the identification and resolution of system factors that impede or prevent meeting customer/client expectations and support the process/project management effort may be added to the above.

Summary

This chapter examined root cause analysis as part of a system. This system includes not only the careful analysis of surfaced problems or unwanted conditions and the development and evaluation of proposed solutions, but also measures that may be taken to determine their effectiveness. This can be reduced to the rather simple question: "Are we discovering the real reasons we have problems and are we taking the appropriate steps to correct and prevent them?"

It is easy to tell when these systems are *not* working. There are lots of problems that appear to need fixing. It also is tempting to continue to apply more fixes until all problems seem to disappear. This can result in most people being too busy fixing and checking to do much else. Time passes and conditions change. So too must the specific treatments administered, as well as the overall program itself. Effective programs evolve and should be allowed to do so.

Root cause analysis, trend analysis, effective corrective and preventive action systems, and others comprise the program called total quality management. For TQM to be effective, all parts or subsystems must be operating smoothly. To ensure this occurs, each of these interlocking systems must be checked occasionally and any adjustments that are needed should be made. This teamwork of systems is as important to achieve TQM as is any other form of activity that requires effective teamwork.

8
CHANGE ANALYSIS

"All is flux, nothing stays still ... Nothing endures but change."

—Heraclitus (540-480 B.C.)

Introduction

Few things in life remain unchanged. Similar to compound interest, change tends to occur at an exponential rather than a linear rate. Changes that took millennia, then centuries, and more recently, generations, are now occurring within lifetimes or even within a matter of years. Consider the example of aviation. It was a little over 80 years ago that the Wright brothers flew those first few feet in their fragile, kitelike craft. Forty years later, the first jets were in the air; and less than 40 years after that, man was walking on the moon. Today, jet travel over great distances is routine to millions of people (some of whom were alive when the Wright brothers first flew). Space shuttle flights go almost unnoticed by many. We take for granted that which would have been considered extraordinary only a short while ago. Computerized cars? Personal computers? Ideas that were the domain of science fiction writers or comic book stories now are routine.

The word "change" has several meanings: making different, altering, transforming, replacing, abandoning, switching. The process of change can affect both systems and people. Change can either reduce or induce personal stress, regardless of whether or not the proposed change is positive or negative in itself. Because of this ability to produce stress, change can create problems. If for no other reason, by transforming environments, change can introduce the potential for problems to occur.

Change analysis is an analytical technique which applies a systematic approach to problem solving by examining the effects of change. Change analysis may be performed in a reactive mode by analyzing unwanted events or problems, or in a proactive mode by identifying the potential effects of changes before they actually are implemented. Change analysis techniques originally were developed at the RAND Corporation and subsequently improved upon by two former RAND employees, Charles H. Kepner and Benjamin B. Tregoe. Change analysis techniques are part of the management oversight and risk tree analysis approach used for event and accident investigations which was developed by EG & G, Idaho, under a contract to a predecessor to the United States Department of Energy.

Introductory Story
Ishmael's company, Pequod Enterprises, recently announced its intention to reorganize its operations. This was prompted by its successful bid for a large contract. The rationale was that, with the reorganization, the company would establish clearer communication channels, since the new organization virtually mirrored that of the client. The new organization consolidated several divisions into new ones and changed a number of reporting and functional responsibilities.

The process of reorganization was not proceeding as smoothly as was originally hoped. Most employees had only heard of the proposed changes through the grapevine. Company management had some problems in lining up the new organization and therefore had not issued a revised organization chart. Recognizing this problem, Ishmael conducted a series of all-employee meetings to sketch out the proposed changes. It was during one of these meetings that Ishmael became aware of yet another problem.

Many employees voiced concerns that, since there had never been any job posting system or other means to change or upgrade their jobs, they were dissatisfied with both their present and proposed new positions. As a means of placating these concerns and ensuring a smoother transition to the new organization, management decided to institute a job survey. Forms were given to each employee, asking them which job they would prefer in the new organization.

Since job descriptions had not yet been prepared for the new positions, there was no pattern to the employee responses. The employees' choices were based on the title as well as the perceived requirements and responsibilities of the position. Recognizing this problem, Ishmael directed his management team to set two priorities: 1) development of new job positions, and 2) definition of responsibilities and authorities of the new organizational units.

The task of defining the mission and function of the new organizational units involved consolidating previous responsibilities and authorities, redistributing others, and adding new ones. In doing this, management began to realize the full impact of the proposed changes. For example, it was discovered that the present mission and function statements, when they existed, were out of date. They all needed revision. Departmental procedures, which described policy and direction, in like fashion, required revision. Virtually all implementing procedures, which detailed day-to-day operations, needed changing. There also were a number of new procedures that needed to be written.

Organized labor also needed to be consulted for impacts on existing labor contracts. Job classification systems needed to be revised and standardized to ensure equity for people performing the same or similar job functions. Existing management systems needed to be evaluated and changed to meet the new organizational needs.

Ishmael was considering his alternatives when an even larger problem surfaced. He received a phone call from the customer's purchasing manager, Hiram Huckley, advising him that a stop work order had been issued on the contract. Citing poor quality and other performance problems, Hiram told Ishmael to cease all activity on the new contract at once and respond, within 30 days, with information on the corrections he intended to make on each of the findings.

Some of the problems Hiram listed were:
- Increased rejection rate of products
- Inattention to client concerns on needed changes
- No correction of identified adverse conditions
- Repeat occurrences of the same problem
- Root causes of problems were not identified
- Problems in identifying exact person responsible to discuss problems or contract progress
- Personnel attitudes judged hostile or nonresponsive

As Ishmael put down the phone, he reflected, "What else can go wrong?" He tried to sort out what to do now. It seemed to him, on the surface, that he had tried to do all the "right" things.

This story will be used later to illustrate the process of change analysis.

Uses for Change Analysis

In its basic form, change analysis defines the cause of events or problems by asking "What has changed?" or "What is different?" that might have directly caused or indirectly precipitated the situation. Change analysis techniques are therefore particularly useful for the following.

Trouble shooting: In trouble shooting, the basic questions "What has changed?" or "What is different?" can quickly help focus a problem.

Finding obscure causes: During the initial stages of an investigation it can be difficult to determine exactly what caused the situation. If all changes and differences are identified (whether they appear to make any difference or not), then whether taken separately or collectively, they may help to gain insight into an otherwise obscure cause.

Analysis of Keystone Kop type activity: Change may result in what could be called Keystone Kop activity. This occurs when otherwise seemingly competent individuals run around in circles without accomplishing much. Some Keystone Kop activity is evident in the introductory story. Knowledgeable and seemingly competent management are trying to operate in a changed situation, but the overall effect has been catastrophic.

Quick entry into problem solving: Change analysis techniques provide a quick-entry systematic approach to solving problems with reasonable credibility. For example, in the introductory story it is relatively easy to list the problems and see the effects caused by change.

It should not be inferred that all changes necessarily create problems. Change, in fact, may be quite necessary and have positive results. Nor do problems resulting from change prove that the old way was better.

Elements of Change

Change influences and thereby puts stress on a system, process, or person. Change, when viewed as an element of change analysis, is that force that can make a difference (positive or negative) in the way a system, process, or person functions. The change can be mandated, occur more or less naturally (whether noticed or not), or be caused (knowingly or not). Changes can be either subtle or pronounced.

Mandated changes result from a variety of intended purposes, including invalid reasoning (change for change's sake) or a need to fulfill the demands of internal or external pressures. Regardless of the change's purpose, problems arise from not properly assessing the impact of the proposed change(s) or not knowing how the change will be implemented or received.

Often, change is implemented because a process, system, or organization appears to need improvement or has gone astray. There is conviction that change is needed and that change will result in improvement. When change is considered because of surfaced problems, it can be termed reactive. When change is considered solely upon the basis of evidence or belief that improvement will result, it can be called proactive. Whether proactive or reactive, effective change must be planned and managed to achieve the desired results.

Change also can occur without being planned. Change can be gradual, like the slight movement of a clock's hands, or it can be sudden, like the turning on or off of a light. Since it occurs slowly, gradual change can be difficult to detect. The effects of gradual change are illustrated in the following story.

Uriah Postulate is a fifth grade math teacher. He has been teaching fifth grade math for 15 years. Uriah had a thorough understanding of math when he graduated from college with a math degree. In fact, his classmates predicted he would become a theoretical mathematician who would eventually rival his famous uncle, Belshazzar Quadratic, who devised the now-famous formula that bears his name. However, the job market for theoretical mathematicians was bleak when Uriah graduated, so he accepted the teaching job until things looked better.

While he taught fifth grade math, his understanding of the more complex math techniques obviously was never put to use. Uriah continued to faithfully read the want ads, looking for just the right position, but one never seemed to come up. Over the years, Uriah's skills in scanning want ads became almost legend, but his ability to understand complex math techniques slowly eroded. One day, Uriah noticed that he was having trouble explaining a particular fifth grade math problem to one of his brighter students, Jeremiah K. Libnite.

What happened? Uriah certainly didn't take any sudden or overt action to lose his competency. Rather, Uriah was the victim of gradual skills decline through disuse. Increased academic requirements for fifth grade math might have pointed out the same problem. The overall students' knowledge base and/or expectations also could have risen to such a level that Uriah could no longer relate to their needs as an instructor.

Uriah's competency level is postulated in Figure 8.1. The plot shows competency level vs. years after graduation. It is reasonable to assume that Uriah initially performed at the college level (since he graduated) and

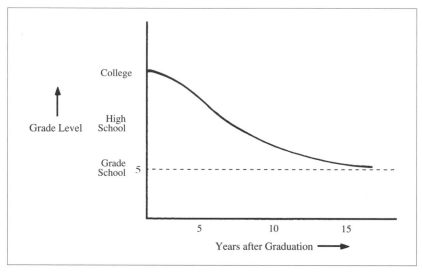

Figure 8.1
Uriah's Math Competency

that his loss of skills probably was greater during the first few years than in later years.

Gradual change can also be evidenced by changed attitudes. A particular service company noticed a decline in contract renewals. It wasn't obvious at first, but the problem was found to be rooted in the attitudes of its service representatives. The more years they had on the job, the less receptive they became to customer requests. In fact, they had formed a sort of fraternity whose informal meetings were spent mostly on discussing the more "outrageous" requests they had received. This desensitivity occurred over a period of time and, like Uriah's math competency, was difficult to detect.

These stories point out that it is sometimes difficult to determine what is changing, even if there is an established reference point. Picture yourself sitting in a train with another train on a track next to you. The other train starts to move very slowly forward in the same direction you are pointing. Lacking any other evidence of movement, it is hard to tell if you are moving backward or the other train is moving forward.

There also is the situation in which an otherwise reliable observation cannot determine *why* change occurred. For example, under special circumstances, quantum theory predicts that a change in an object in one place can instantly produce a change in (another) related object somewhere else—even on the other side of the universe. Suppose now you were on that other side of the universe trying to explain this change without the benefit of what was just told you. As part of the process of change analysis, these cause and effect relationships are formed. To the extent these inferred relationships are not accurate, the overall analysis is flawed.

The biggest problem is that most events or problems involve people. The investigator or analyst must be alert to the reality that people are complex creatures. People do not always move in straight lines or in a predictable fashion, nor respond to change in the same way.

Implementation

Another element of change analysis is the manner in which change was implemented. For those planning or implementing change, sound advice might be that which is also given physicians (Hippocratic oath): "First do no harm." When analyzing how change is implemented, it is helpful to ask the following questions:

Was change implemented in a timely fashion? If certain changes are made too slowly, the dynamics of the process or environment may nullify the effects of change. Changes implemented at an inappropriate time may escalate the event situation. If changes are made too quickly, other problems arise. This begs the question "What is the proper timing?" Timing is a crucial decision that must be made during the planning phase. Allowance must be made for system lags and other factors.

The process of introducing and implementing change is depicted in Figure 8.2. Two aspects are shown to be important: the amount of desired change and its timing.

The initiation of the desired change is shown as time zero (t_0). It is desired that the change be fully implemented at some point in the future,

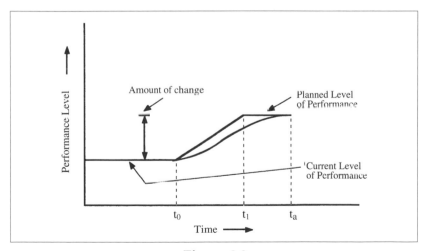

Figure 8.2
Implementing Change

shown as t_1. The normal system response time, however, might be longer. This is shown as t_a, the actual time required for the system to accommodate the change. Unless this system response time was factored into the planning efforts, it should be obvious that there will be problems. Ishmael's company did not appear to factor in any settling in time. In real life, many organizations do not factor this normal response time in planning changes. To reduce this natural response time, changes in the system itself probably will be required. The magnitude of the proposed change will also directly influence the normal system response time. Most systems have self-correcting mechanisms to allow for minor changes.

Other questions related to implementation are:

What is the amount of proposed change? As has already been suggested, the amount or degree of proposed change needs to be considered. To determine this, the present level or condition (baseline) must be known. What was the starting point? Do you know what you had originally? Can you return if need be? How might you keep from returning?

Was the implementation complete? If complete, does it meet the intended objectives? Changes need to be considered in their total context. The objectives need to be carefully examined to ensure they will produce the desired effect. For example, implementing a manufacturing award program that includes only production personnel might cause dissatisfaction among others who feel unfairly excluded, such as purchasing personnel. The efforts of these personnel might be clearly as important to increased production. It is not difficult to predict that such an incomplete initiative might be counterproductive and even impair production in the long run.

Were reinforcing factors considered and included as part of change implementation? Reinforcing factors include those steps taken to ensure that changed ways of doing business remain changed. It is very easy to slip back into the older, more familiar ways of doing business. Installing appropriate pulse points to monitor how well the desired change remains in effect is a good practice. The reader is reminded of the discussion of these and other validation concepts in Chapter 3.

An example of how easy it is to slip back into old habits can be demonstrated by Ezekiel Gommorah. Fed up with paying for two seats on every airline flight, Ezekiel decided the time was ripe for a serious attempt to shed a few pounds.

After consulting with his physician, Ezekiel enthusiastically launched his diet program. His eating and exercise habits were dramatically changed. Following the program, Ezekiel reached his goal. Both Ezekiel and his doctor were immensely pleased with his progress. Ezekiel was so pleased, in fact, he decided to celebrate with one of his old passions: a banana split with all the fixings in front of the TV. After all, didn't he deserve it?

Resistance to Change

Most people do not like change. It is an intrusion on their comfortable, steady-state environment. They have been accustomed to doing things in certain ways. People prefer to do things the same way each time because it took some time to learn to do it this way and they resist having to learn all over again. Even if the proposed change makes sense, they may reject it simply because it wasn't their idea.

Some of the reasons change is resisted follow:

Lack of vision: If people do not know the purpose behind implementing the change or of what the change will consist, they are likely to resist.

Lack of commitment: If key individuals do not show support for proposed change through words, actions, and personal involvement, interest in the change will quickly die.

Culture: If the organizational or social culture doesn't encourage change, the change will be resisted.

Structural support: The organization may not be able to facilitate change because of its structure. For example, the company may want to resolve employee concerns, but if there is no organization in place for employees to raise their concerns, the concept may prove self-defeating.

Personal threat: If people view the change as harming their status, position, or control, they will resist.

Incentive: If the payoffs or consequences for change don't outweigh the status quo, resistance usually wins over the incentive to change.

Information: If information involving the change is incorrect, inadequate, or constantly changing, the change could be thought of as ill-conceived.

Involvement and control: If people who will be affected by the change are not involved, there will be resistance to change. People like to think that they have some control over their own destinies.

Fear of the unknown: If change contains too many unknowns or risks, people may hold fast to the comfort of an existing way of doing business.

Extra work: If the change is likely to change a person's comfortable lifestyle by inducing extra work or effort, it will be resisted, especially if the incentives for change don't outweigh the extra work involved.

Resources: If the available resources are inadequate to accomplish change, there will be lack of support for the change.

Timing: Change will be resisted if there is a lack of readiness for the change, or matters of higher priority keep putting off change.

Political uncertainty: Some people will hold off supporting change until they can determine the direction the change will take and the appropriateness of responses. This is commonly referred to as the Good Old Boy syndrome.

Another reason people resist any change is that there are too many options to consider. For example, consider the television industry. When TV was first introduced, there were only a few channels from which to choose. As the years passed, more TV channels were introduced. Today there are literally hundreds of channels from which to choose. A person could easily spend an entire hour flipping through different channels or studying the television guides trying to find the station they really want to watch and end up viewing nothing. Overwhelmed by the choices, some will choose not to turn the channel at all, thereby avoiding making any decision.

Evaluating Change

Proposed changes, based solely on inherent merit, can be worthwhile, worthless, or something in between. The planning and implementation of change also can be measured and judged adequate or inadequate.

A simple change evaluation matrix can help. Consider the two variables listed above (the idea itself vs. its planning and implementation) as well as their condition (whether positive or negative, adequate or less than adequate). Placing these in a matrix (Table 8.1) provides a means for predicting outcomes.

It can be seen that two of the above combinations of idea and implementation yield questionable results. When the idea is positive but the planning or implementation is negative, revising the plan, strengthening

	PLANNING AND IMPLEMENTATION EFFECTIVE	PLANNING AND IMPLEMENTATION LESS THAN ADEQUATE
GOOD IDEA	Results of change good	Questionable results
POOR IDEA	Questionable results	Results of change bad

Table 8.1
Matrix of "Predictable" Outcomes

some element of implementation, or overcoming resistance to change may result in a positive outcome.

In the other case, the idea was negative but implementation was positive. Taking a second look at the idea is definitely in order. Perhaps modifying the idea will make the proposed change more saleable.

In some cases, it might be desirable to further quantify the expected results of proposed changes. If the proposed change is large or costly, then predicting its results using a more formal model may be appropriate.

Based on the discussion so far, the following relatively simple model could be constructed:

Expected results = (Weighting factor x merit of change) ± (Weighting factor x planning and/or implementation aspects).

The weighting factors chosen will depend on the organization. Certain organizations (e.g., banks holding fiduciary, public, or other trust) might assign weighting factors to planning and/or implementation aspects that will be large compared to those assigned to the merit of change. In other words, even small changes will be subject to considerable planning and gradual cautious implementation. This is, of course, entirely appropriate to their situation. High-tech companies, on the other hand, might assign higher weighting factors to the merit of change, since they must follow trends more rapidly and closely.

Since there can be many changes, planning, and implementation factors occurring at any given time in most organizations, a more complex model might be considered. Change can be thought of (in the same mathematical terms) as a multiple linear regression equation where all variables and effects on the outcome can be analyzed. Expressed in mathematical terms:

$$R = \pm A_1 (X_1) \perp A_2(X_2) \pm A_3(X_3) \dots A_n(X_n), \text{ where}$$

$A_1 \dots A_n$ are weighting factors and $X_1 \dots X_n$ are variables.

The expected results of change on the overall organization is therefore the sum of variable 1 ± variable 2 ± variable 3, and so forth. The above model can be made even more elaborate by including probabilities; for those interested in this subject, the construction and testing of math models is covered in any number of management science, mathematical, and statistical texts.

Process of Reactive Change Analysis

Change analysis determines the root cause of the event by examining the effects of change, assigning individual causes, and then determining the root cause by either isolating the predominant cause or identifying one cause (the trigger) which, if corrected or avoided, would have prevented the problem from occurring.

The first step in the analysis process is to identify *all* observed and perceived changes. Each change must be defined and isolated for subsequent evaluation. Often this is difficult to do. Experience in safety-related events has shown that there usually are a number of change factors and hence potential causes.

For example, consider the simple case of an automobile accident in which there is only one vehicle involved which skids off the road. When the police arrive, the driver is noticeably intoxicated. The obvious conclusion given the clues thus far is that the accident was caused by the driver's condition.

In truth, the driver may have taken one or several drinks only *after* the accident and not before. There may have been a slick condition, which might have caused the accident regardless of the driver's condition. Or an animal which leapt onto the road was avoided. Maybe there was a poorly lighted unmarked curve or bump which temporarily caused the car to go out of control. This list of other possible causal factors could be expanded, but the point is obvious. The listing of changed circumstances and their possible effect must be as complete as possible. If a factor is missing, the analysis can be seriously flawed or totally inaccurate.

This same problem exists when performing events and causal factors analysis. The analyst must be reasonably clear of all the aspects of change and how these differences relate to the problem at hand. Change analysis is a relatively simple technique, which turns out to be both its strength and weakness.

Each deviation (change) observed or suspected should be listed and described separately. Observed (actual) changes noted should be precisely defined and described by identity, location, time, and extent. The what, where, when, and how questions which are drilled into all cub reporters on their first day on the job are an excellent guide in constructing the analysis.

Change analysis is most easily conducted using a change analysis worksheet, such as that illustrated in Figure 8.3. This worksheet can be tailored as needs arise and made as cursory or comprehensive as the analyst feels is necessary to accomplish the task. The worksheet is shown with the suggested who, what, when, where, and how questions listed as a starting point. Some organizations have found it helpful to add other standard factors such as installed controls, working conditions, extent of problem, job or task statement, schedule, procedures, personnel, tools, supervision, etc. The point is that the worksheet should list all factors appropriate to the situation or organization.

The next question that may arise is the amount of information that should be obtained and entered for each of the listed factors. There is no hard and fast rule for this, but experience suggests that the preliminary worksheet should contain as much detail and list as many possible changes or differences (potential causes) that are observed or suspected.

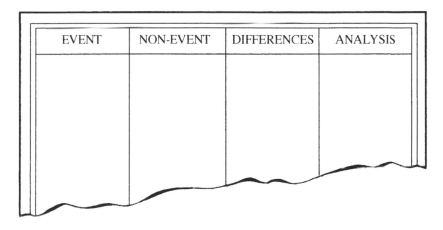

Figure 8.3
Typical Change Analysis Worksheet

Those familiar with the process prefer to let the subsequent analysis identify factors that do not need to be included or further examined. This practice reduces the possibility of overlooking what may later prove to be the most obvious reason.

The process of reactive change analysis consists of six basic steps:

1. **Describe the event situation.** Describe the event situation or problem as precisely as possible. In accident or problem event investigation, the situation usually is quite clear. Describe who was involved, what was involved, where the event took place, when the event took place, and how or what might have enabled the event to take place. Be objective and avoid biasing; make sure all possible factors are included.

2. **Describe an event-free or non-event situation.** Describe a non-event, or the situation without problems. The non-event should be given the same considerations as the event, as far as describing it in

terms of who, what, where, when, and how. As much as possible, avoid automatically making it a not or inverse of the preceding list. For example, in our single-car accident, if driver inebriation was listed in step 1, then sobriety could be listed in this step using a simple not (not inebriated). The problem in logic that will arise later, however, is that reduced faculties or responsiveness (which may be the cause) is excluded from sobriety. For example, reduced faculties could result from fatigue.

3. **Compare the two.** Compare the two situations to detect any differences. This involves examining each of the elements (who, what, where, when, and how) and asking the question, "How do these two situations *really* differ from each other?"

4. **Write down all detected differences.** Write down all detected differences that set the event situation apart from the uneventful situation.

5. **Analyze the difference.** Analyze these differences to identify underlying causes and describe how they influenced the event. Try each noted difference and assigned cause or influence for effect. Would this change or difference explain the result? Try it in a simple sentence: "Since (or because) . . . *cause,* the . . . *event or problem* . . . occurred, otherwise it would have resulted in a . . . *nonevent.*" If problems in logic are noted, it may be necessary to revisit steps 1 and 2 to make any needed changes or redefinitions. Be sure to look for obscure and indirect relationships, as well as any synergism that may exist.

6. **Integrate information and specify root cause.** Integrate the results of the change analysis. A useful technique is to assign a preliminary cause as each row of the matrix is completed. When the final analysis is conducted, the analyst can utilize either the predominant or trigger approach to identify the true or actual root cause. The predominant approach utilizes the preliminary cause that appears most often or exclusively. The trigger approach involves further retrospect, to identify the primary cause by the logic that, if *this* cause was eliminated, the event would not have occurred. Since the event or problem did not occur, all other causes are moot (need not be considered).

Through the discipline of the analysis matrix, the change-based analysis can lead to a thorough examination of deficiencies, as introduced by changes in personnel, plant and hardware, procedures, and managerial controls. Changes from a previous non-event experience are often subtle, but the information is there for an investigator to construct a careful analysis.

Some Practical Advice

Some analysts prefer to construct the change analysis worksheet differently. Instead of completing the worksheet on a line-by-line basis as suggested above, they first list all identified aspects of the problem. The non-event column is then completed, with conditions that are or have not been changed noted in the difference and analysis columns. The entire worksheet is completed in a columnar fashion. No particular advantage (nor disadvantage) is claimed for this approach. Properly done, the same results should be obtained.

The following are some practical pointers and advice which apply using either approach. The first deals with the importance of listing all possible factors and potential change situations. Do not arbitrarily decide that a factor may not be important. It is better to let the change analysis process itself weed out those changes that did not impact or cause the problem or event. This practice will eliminate possible oversights.

Another helpful practice is to either construct some additional columns or make notes to the side of each row entry for two items: the need for any counterchange noted as a result of examining the factor and the apparent cause for that particular line item. The former will be helpful in framing solutions later as well as in identifying current system or program flaws. The latter (apparent cause) will be useful in the final synthesis of the root cause. By noting the apparent causes as you go along, you can later look for any resultant pattern or trigger cause.

Another question that arises is that of the specificity required for the non-event. In most cases, it is described as the lack of the event under consideration, sort of changing all the signs to + or listing it as the "good twin." This, of course, implies that the lack of a problem is a desirable condition or state of events, which is faulty logic. In certain problem situations, the non-event may be difficult to construct or visualize. The remedy for this concern lies in re-examination of the basic change analysis technique itself. Change analysis analyzes the effect of changes or differences. Circumstances related to the event itself certainly are well known. The real reason for comparing this with a non-event is primarily to identify and list these differences. Once this is done, the analysis can proceed. Even if a past practice is not known, but there is a suspected difference, the analysis may continue using this information. The authors recommend that whenever this is done, the information which represents an assumption or has not been verified be clearly noted. Obviously, if the subsequent analysis confirms this piece to be important, it will need to be checked.

Pequod Enterprises

To illustrate the application of change analysis techniques, let's return to the story at the beginning of this chapter. In this example, inadequate management, particularly lack of planning, appeared to be the root cause. At this point, however, this would be a subjective judgment. The change analysis worksheet constructed for the introductory story, with an explanation of each of the line entries provided, is shown in Figure 8.4 and its accompanying notes.

EVENT	NON-EVENT	DIFFERENCES	ANALYSIS
Reorganization problems (1)	Smoother transition (2)	Major changes, personnel confused (3)	Planning less than adequate (4)
Reorganization problems (5)	Adequate plan (6)	Responsibilities not clear (7)	Confusion (8)
New contract (9)	Adequate plan (10)	Reorganization (11)	Smoother transition (12)
Lack of plan (13)	Adequate plan (14)	Existing plan (15)	Planning less than adequate (16)

Figure 8.4
Change Analysis–Pequod Enterprises
(Numbers refer to notes below)

Note 1. In the introductory story, Ishmael's company, Pequod Enterprises, had just received a new, large contract. In an effort to re-align his company with that of the new customer organization, he decided on a major internal reorganization.

Note 2. Ishmael could have planned for a smoother transition and thereby avoided at least some of the problems encountered during the reorganization. He also could have created a separate interface unit until the reorganization was up and running. Another alternative might have been to make some minor changes to match the customer organization, with others to follow. He may have overlooked the natural response time of the organization to accommodate changes, especially major ones.

Note 3. The difference resulting from this less than adequate planning and implementation were organizational problems and individuals who were unsure of their new responsibilities.

Note 4. The analysis is that there appeared to be little planning provided for the reorganization. It was not until the second major setback, that of the employee concerns, was encountered, that the company realized just how much effort reorganization would require. The conclusion is obvious: planning and implementation were less than adequate.

Note 5. This row looks more at the *what* of the situation. Once again, as in Note 1, the event situation is the reorganization attempt.

Note 6. A non-event situation in this case looks beyond the reorganization, to the fact that it was not the reorganization itself that caused problems but the lack of an adequate plan and effective implementation thereof. It was only toward the end of the introductory story (and then too late) that any sort of planned actions were considered.

Note 7. From the customer's findings, it is obvious that personnel were generally unaware of their responsibilities in the new organization. There are a number of problems, such as the product defects, that apparently were not corrected in a timely fashion. To fully support this assumption, further investigation would be required.

Note 8. There exists little doubt, however, that considerable confusion existed in employees' minds as to their roles in the new organization. The fact that little specific information had been supplied did little to encourage personnel to assume "that's my responsibility."

Note 9. This row explores the *when* aspect. The triggering event was the award of the new contract. Had this not occurred, the problem might not have surfaced, at least in the fashion and to the degree that it did.

Note 10. Given the award of the new contract, a non-event situation might have occurred if, during the bid phases, Ishmael's firm had considered the full impact of the contract. The need to consider a reorganization might not have been evident, but it was important enough to consider once the award was announced.

Note 11. Had plans been made, the new organization might have been successfully accomplished.

Note 12. If management plans had been adequate, then the transition would probably have been smoother. Many of the problems associated with change (see previous discussion in text) could have either been avoided or dealt with in advance.

Note 13. This row deals with the *how* questions. It is apparent by now that the problem arose primarily because of the lack of a well-thought-out contingency plan should the contract be awarded. Almost all that was done was based on reaction. It could be argued that trying to solve a second problem before the first had been satisfactorily resolved only further complicated the situation. Trying to effect a reorganization with all its attendant problems (even *with* a reasonable plan) and, at the same time, allowing personnel to play musical chairs was almost a sure recipe for disaster.

Note 14. It can be presumed that an adequate plan might have mitigated some of the problems encountered.

Note 15. The overall analysis is that lack of planning (part of management methods) was the major reason problems were encountered. If the listing provided in Chapter 3 is reviewed, the root cause Change Management emerges as the proper choice, since this refers to management methods during the change process, which is the case here.

If informal causes had been assigned as each row was completed, the results might have been as follows:

Row 1 (Notes 1–4): lack of planning

Row 2 (Notes 5–8): less than adequate communication

Row 3 (Notes 9–12): lack of planning

Row 4 (Notes 13–16): lack of planning

It can be seen that lack of planning dominates the list. In fact, the less than adequate communication cause (Row 2) can be attributed to the fact that there was nothing to tell—no plan to disclose. So the overall (predominant) cause was lack of planning. Since planning is a management responsibility, review of the causes listed in Chapter 3 reveals the specific change management root cause assigned—chosen because this addresses is the management process during change.

The Prospective Process

Change analysis, as described so far, refers to analyzing events for those conditions that were changed (or somehow different) and then analyzing their effect to determine the real reason the event occurred. This has been termed reactive root cause analysis.

These same basic techniques can also be used in the forward or prospective mode. Prospective change analysis predicts the effects of change. It can be used to study the effects of change on a process, system, or organization to reveal potential event situations before these changes are actually made.

Prospective change analysis, in the same fashion as the technique used in a reactive mode, looks at and defines the who, what, where, when, and how of change.

The process of prospective change analysis can be described in four steps.

1. **The present situation.** Describe the present situation. Describe who will be affected by the change, what will change, where the change will take place, when the change will take place, and how the change will be implemented.

2. **Planned changes.** All of the planned changes should be described in terms of people, locations, materials, processes, and proposed barriers and controls. See Chapter 9.

3. **Effects of planned changes.** List all known or potential effects of the proposed changes.

4. **Evaluate the results.** Analyze the potential effects and summarize the results to provide the final evaluation of the proposed changes.

Prospective change analysis is useful for change control. By change control, it is not implied that it is possible to control change, but only that the effect of changes can be controlled. This means that changes should be subjected to this technique as a means of mitigating or avoiding potential problems. As pointed out throughout this book, the most expensive or regrettable events or problems are those that could have been avoided.

Summary

Change and the resulting resistance to change can cause problems. Even planned, effective changes can lead to problems if not properly implemented. Change analysis analyzes the root cause of problems by examining what is different and the effect of this difference.

Change analysis can be used as both a proactive and reactive tool. It is a relatively straightforward step-by-step process which focuses on change elements and their effect. It allows easy entry into problem analysis and is effective when other techniques do not work as well.

Disadvantages of change analysis include the risk of finding the obvious (but wrong) answer to events or problems, as in our example of the drunk driver. In certain situations, so many things may have changed that it may be hard to get a handle on the problem using this approach. In other cases, the effects of change may not be perceptible because the change has occurred so slowly or there are simply too many changes to be considered.

Change analysis is perhaps the simplest of all the formal root cause analysis techniques and that most likely to be influenced by subjectivity or bias. For this reason, on problems of a more serious nature, change analysis works best as an entry to the process or as a check on another root cause analysis technique.

9
BARRIER ANALYSIS

A sign on a fence reads:

"While it takes the average person one minute to
run across this field, it takes my bull only 59 seconds."

—Example of a barrier by the authors

Introduction

An unwanted event, incident, accident, or problem can be considered as the result of a number of different elements coming together in a certain fashion. Considered separately or together in some other combination, in slightly differing degree or displaced in time, these same elements might otherwise produce no noticeable adverse outcome. When these elements are known (or suspected) to have the potential to cause an unwanted event or problem, safeguards or barriers may be installed to prevent this from happening. Barrier analysis looks at these potential sources of problems or hazards as well as how the harm or damage occurred. It also examines any possible interaction(s) and determines the root cause of the problem or unwanted event by assessing the adequacy of any installed barriers or safeguards that should have prevented, or at least mitigated, its occurrence.

Barrier analysis techniques can be used to examine administrative and procedural problems, equipment or system failures, injuries, accidents, and other similar events. Barrier analysis offers users the advantages of a well-defined root cause analysis technique which provides reasonably reproducible results. The focus is, of course, on those barriers or safeguards that should have prevented or mitigated the unwanted event or problem.

Barrier analysis normally is used in a reactive mode to solve surfaced problems or investigate events. However, the technique lends itself to conducting a proactive evaluation of existing barriers as well as helping to identify additional barriers that might be considered. Barrier analysis also can help to identify missing safeguards, those that might have prevented the problem *if they had been in place.* This suggests barrier analysis may also be useful in a proactive mode, i.e., to identify additional safeguards that should be considered to prevent recurrence.

Barrier analysis techniques also can be utilized to examine existing barriers even though a problem has not yet occurred. Postulated events can be used to examine the adequacy of existing barriers. Proposed additional barriers can then be devised to prevent (or at least mitigate) these undesirable events. Load testing is one physical example in which simulated conditions are used to confirm design calculations. Readiness reviews, constructability or manufacturability reviews, system checks, war games, flight simulators, and other activities can also be considered as forms of proactive barrier analysis.

In this chapter, we will examine the basic elements of barrier analysis as well as the various types of barriers, clearly distinguishing between those that may be considered hard and soft. To illustrate these concepts, we begin with the story of Elmo S. Fiero, farm worker.

Introductory Story
In farming, irrigation of the crop sometimes is accomplished by mechanical means. The water distribution system may be permanently installed or provided by temporary irrigation lines (since these have the advantages of lower initial cost and operational flexibility).

One of the field irrigator's normal jobs is to change these hand irrigation lines, commonly called handlines. Even though these pipes can be quite long (40 feet), they are reasonably lightweight since they are usually made from aluminum. When repositioning handlines, irrigators often lift one end to allow any water left in the pipe to drain out. If lifted too high, there is a potential for the aluminum pipe to come in contact with overhead obstructions, such as trees or power lines.

Elmo S. Fiero, an employee on a relatively large farm, was changing handlines next to some overhead power lines. While performing this task he upended a handline which, unfortunately, came into contact with an overhead transmission line. As a result, electricity flowed down the metal handline and through Elmo, giving him a real jolt. Other workers noticed the brilliant flash and rushed to his aid. Elmo was hospitalized with severe burns. Just prior to the accident, Elmo had received safety training, which included the dangers of uplifting handlines near power lines. For years, this training had been given to employees prior to and during the growing season. With many years of safe operations, the farm was considered by many to be the best in the business.

It was common practice, as well as the farm's stated safety requirement, to use the buddy system while changing lines. This practice helped ensure that employees didn't injure themselves while lifting and moving lines, and provided an extra pair of eyes to help watch for overhead hazards. On this particular day Elmo's helper, Tessler Coyle, was ill and absent from work. Elmo, however, had decided to perform the work by himself rather than notify the supervisor and be assigned another partner or forced to do other chores. "It may have been a bad decision," he later admitted. Upon discharge from the hospital, Elmo never returned to farm work, claiming it was too dangerous, and went to work for the power company as a lineman.

As in the previous chapter, this story will be used later to illustrate the concept of barrier analysis.

Elements

Barrier analysis defines the basic elements of an unwanted event or problem as the following.

- Threats, hazards, or forces that could adversely influence the state or condition of things of value (appropriately referred to as the targets)
- The targets or things of value themselves
- Barriers or safeguards that are supposed to keep the threats from coming into contact with the targets
- The trace of the threats' contact with or influence on the target as evidenced by the occurrence of the undesirable event or problem

For the purpose of this text, the words *event* and *incident* will be used in specific ways. An incident is considered to be an event where a barrier designed to prevent a threat from reaching a target fails, but the barrier's failure does not result in any loss or undesirable consequence. An event or problem is always associated with adverse consequences. Of course, often the difference is a matter of degree.

Based on these definitions, the following four elements are considered in a barrier analysis of an event or problem:

1. The threat that does the harm
2. The people or thing (target) that is harmed
3. The barrier(s) that could have or should have prevented the threat from reaching the target
4. The path or trace by which the threat reached the target

An incident usually will only involve analyzing items 1 (threat) and 3 (barrier). It should also be pointed out that while it is easiest to describe barrier analysis techniques by discussing the elements in the order shown, during the actual analysis, it often is more convenient to proceed by first defining the target that is damaged (2), identifying the source (1), the transmission mode (4), and then identifying and assessing the adequacy of any barriers (3).

Threats

Threats, by definition, are those things or conditions that have the potential to cause harm or an adverse outcome. We will use the terms *threat, hazard,* and *potential problem* source somewhat interchangeably throughout this chapter, but the meaning should be clear to the reader. These threats are all around us. Some are easily recognized by one or several senses (e.g., seeing *and* hearing an airplane propeller or spinning saw blade).

Other threats are recognized through experience or learning (e.g., a bare electrical wire or sharp knife). Lacking the motion of the previous examples or otherwise obvious signals through the senses, they are no less potent sources for harm. Other threats can come from seemingly harmless sources. In addition to his remarkable story-telling abilities, the true genius of Stephen King lies in his ability to create menace using everyday things, such as an old automobile (Christine). He rarely invokes horror using obvious means such as hoary monsters from some dismal swamp. The point here is that threats *can* come from otherwise unexpected sources. Many children are hurt every year using toys, intended for the child's pleasure.

During recent years, technology has advanced rapidly. Producing numerous benefits, it also has produced a great number of threats. Ideally, when a new product or technology is introduced, means to detect, alarm, or protect us from embedded or potential threats should be considered. However, this is not always the case, and we must continually learn new ways to live with our technology and protect ourselves from any dangers it may introduce, as well as fending against all previous and naturally occurring threats.

Most of the threats considered in barrier analysis will be described in terms of energy, specifically its manifestation as kinetic energy. Although the source of the threat may be described in terms of its potential (energy), the problem or unwanted event occurs when this energy is transformed or delivered. Energy may be said to exist and be delivered in two basic forms. The desirable form is controlled energy; the non-desired form is unwanted or uncontrolled energy. Controlled energy produces desired results in a predictable fashion. Unwanted energy can produce an undesirable result directly or an unwanted by-product during a (seemingly) desirable or controlled transformation of energy.

Energy sources include chemical, biological, thermal, electrical, and ionizing and non-ionizing radiation. Energy can be described in terms of social and economic forces, religious and humanistic beliefs, the environment, the political climate, economic conditions, and other similar conditions.

A transfer of energy released in such a way, amount, or rate that it influences targets or things of value in unexpected or unwanted ways (e.g., in an accident) is cause for concern. When used in a proactive mode, barrier analysis looks at how potentially harmful effects of energy can be effectively managed to prevent the unwanted transference of energy to targets.

Going back to the introductory example, electricity is meant to flow through power lines to homes and factories for desired uses, such as making toast or smelting steel. It is not intended to flow through an irrigation pipe (and the person holding it) to the ground. In this example, the threat was the electricity and the target was the person injured by contact with it through the pipe, which is not considered the normal delivery means or path for this energy.

Threats then are real or potentially harmful sources of energies which can produce adverse effects on targets or things of value. The forms which these threats or hazards may take are limitless.

Targets
Targets are defined as those things of value harmed, degraded, or otherwise adversely affected as a result of coming into contact with the threat. The logical starting point in thinking about targets focuses on persons and objects. In a larger sense, however, things of value can include institutions, places, social or economic conditions, status, goodwill, friendships, etc. When you consider this, the list is endless.

As previously pointed out, when performing barrier analysis, the targets usually are listed first. It is good practice to initially list *all* potential targets, and then, as the analysis proceeds, eliminate those targets that were not affected by the undesirable event or problem.

People: As targets, people can be thought of either individually or collectively as a group. People can be grouped by proximity to one another (i.e., work groups or neighborhoods) or by association based on other factors (i.e., profession).

In the example of the field irrigator, the target was the irrigator who upended the irrigation pipe into the power line. In this case the transfer of electrical power to the irrigator injured him severely. Other people who might be considered as potential targets damaged as a result of the accident include the direct supervisor who may be judged lax in overview, the person who performed the training which may now be regarded as ineffective, and the farm manager or owner who may suffer financial loss. The other farm workers might also be affected if, as a result of subsequent actions, the operation is closed.

Things: Things are easy to visualize. You can touch, see, smell, or hear things such as cars, a house or building, piping and electrical circuitry, and equipment. It also is fairly easy to assess damage done by threats or hazards to targets you can touch, see, taste, or otherwise sense. When a car accident occurs, it is easy to see the harm that was done (i.e., bent fenders, smashed radiators, broken glass).

As with people, things may be considered in a collective sense. The steel industry can be thought of as an assemblage of the capital equipment, raw material, finished product, sub-suppliers, etc., comprising this activity. The definition of steel industry might be further expanded if it is meant to include not only the above "things" but also persons working in, relying on, affected by, or otherwise associated with this industry segment.

Things can be other than material. For example, goodwill is another thing of value that can be affected by unwanted threats. A classic case is the Tylenol™ scare in the early 1980s. The introduction of poison into this product affected the company's name (goodwill) and position in the marketplace. Eventually, some good did result from this event. Requirements for tamper-proof containers were developed and instituted, not only for Tylenol™ products, but also for a number of other consumer goods.

The Environment: The environment is thought of in terms of air, water, soil, and other parts of our ecosystem: the air we breathe, the water we drink, and the earth on which we walk. In a broader sense, however, the environment also includes political, socioeconomic, philosophical, and religious systems. These systems also can be affected in adverse ways if they come in contact with threats.

An event at a large chemical facility may result in contamination to the air, soil, and water in its vicinity. It might also cause the closure of the chemical production facilities, which could affect the economy of an area, as well as affecting local, national, or even international politics. Consider the Bhopal incident or the Chernobyl disaster. The Chernobyl incident devastated large regions of the Soviet Union. There were losses of lives and equipment. In a larger sense, however, the Chernobyl accident affected operations of all nuclear facilities throughout the world. In the United States, the event resulted in further aggravation to the commercial nuclear power generation industry, which was already ailing as the result of the Three Mile Island accident.

Barriers

So far we have discussed targets and threats. Since things of value (targets) can be harmed, degraded, or otherwise adversely affected when they come into contact with the threat, it seems obvious that the easiest solution is that these two be held apart or kept separated (as by space, time, or other means). If they cannot be kept separate, then the potential flow of energy between the two might somehow be limited to acceptable levels, the target itself strengthened, or other precautions taken to minimize the possibility of an event occurring. The overall intent of these preventive measures is to safely enclose the threat or provide other safeguards to keep the threat from reaching the targets. Barriers, therefore, are those things that prevent passage, approach, or control, and/or minimize the impact of unwanted contact between threats and targets. For example, many animals utilize visual or audible warnings of the danger they represent, such as the gaudily marked poisonous tree frogs or the warning signal of the rattlesnake.

Barriers are put into place to regulate or confine the potentially harmful effects of a process, i.e., to control unwanted energy flow. Examples include flow and pressure regulators, containment vessels, training, and work procedures. Protective clothing (e.g., fire-resistant gloves, masks and coveralls, safety training, emergency plans, pulley guards, and hand rails) are also barriers. Control rods in a nuclear reactor regulate the fission. They also are a safety device in that during a shutdown they are fully inserted into the nuclear core, preventing further reaction.

There are a number of ways that hazards and targets may be prevented from coming into contact with each other including the following:

Eliminate the hazard. Prevent or preclude the existence or manufacture of the threat or energy. Use alternative or safer sources.

Reduce the hazard. Reduce the amount of uncontrolled available energy. Moderate or reduce the amount or degree of the threat in some fashion. Spread or distribute the risk or total amount of danger or hazard. Limit voltages and volumes of hazardous or inflammable material. Use other materials.

Modify the release. Modify or alter the rate of the threat's release. Avoid high compression forces; an example might be reduction of the air supply pressure or the intrinsically safe electric devices used in explosive atmospheres. Divert the release.

Separate in time or space. Isolate or separate targets and threats by time and/or space. An example of this is the time and distance considerations in ALARA (As Low As Reasonably Achievable) radiation protection concepts. Another example is the clearing of harbors and avoidance of vessel movement during normal office or rush hours by LNG (Liquified Natural Gas) tankers.

Isolate the targets or hazards. Enclose or surround either the threat or the target. An example is the containment structure for a nuclear reactor; another is insulation on electrical wires. Fence off or limit access. Post signs.

Strengthen the target. Strengthen or otherwise make the target able to withstand the effects of the threat (e.g., installing shatterproof glass in automobiles). Other examples include bulletproof vests, protective clothing, safety glasses, and earthquake-proof building designs.

Reduce the effect. Install mitigating devices to reduce the effect of an unwanted event or problem. For example, install air bags in automobiles to reduce fatalities or continuous air monitoring systems in facilities that have the potential for airborne chemical or radiological contamination.

The above suggestions can be considered and used singly or in combination, in series or in parallel. The listing also may be used to identify barriers that are not currently used but might be considered. Depending on the particular situation, however, some may be impractical. For example, consider the first strategy listed, that of preventing or precluding the manufacture of the threat. Not producing or manufacturing the potential threat or hazard is a negative, avoidance approach.

In the example, the electric power supplied is required and used in the farm operations; elimination of the energy source is not a realistic option. So other barriers, such as separation of the energy and potential targets, are utilized. Normally power is carried in lines high enough above the ground for most postulated accident scenarios, although obviously not the one in the story. If the use of an extremely long conductor (such as the pipe, a construction crane, or other such item) were to be considered, the lines could be raised higher. It may not make sense to do this routinely, however, since higher lines pose other problems. Putting them underground would have prevented the accident in the story, but like raising the lines higher, other hazards and possible accident scenarios may be introduced. In some situations, such as lowering the flash point of fuels to reduce the danger of fires or explosion, there may be an unacceptable tradeoff in engine efficiency.

The above examples point out important features in barriers. First, a barrier designed in a certain manner may not preclude *all* possible means in which the energy and target may come together and devising an alternate barrier may introduce new potential event situations. Second, certain barriers may be put into place in a limited fashion with reliance placed on other barriers to complete the desired protection.

Barriers are further categorized into being either physical (hard) or administrative (soft).

Physical Barriers

Physical barriers include such items as seat belts and air bags in a car, insulation on electrical wiring, pop-off valves on a pressure vessel, the containment vessel around a nuclear reactor, and warning devices placed on equipment or processes. Physical barriers are either intrinsic or extrinsic. In the best of possible worlds, all required barriers would be intrinsic, designed into the process or final product. Fisher-Price toys provide a good example of designed in or intrinsic barriers. Fisher-Price spends a great deal of time and effort trying to make their toys kidproof. They purposely destroy toys to test for potential faults which might cause laceration, fragmentation, ingestion, asphyxiation, or other harmful effects upon children.

Extrinsic barriers can be used to reduce the effects of threats that cannot be easily eliminated through design. This includes safeguards, interlocks, warning devices, etc. Extrinsic barriers are appropriate when it is not possible to prevent the existence of threats by an intrinsic means. Alarms, for instance, generate warning signals to alert users, operators, or others (e.g., passersby) of the potential occurrence of unwanted events. An example is the alarm that sounds every time certain vehicles are placed in reverse gear. When the transmission is placed in reverse, this alarm sounds to alert people in the vicinity that a vehicle is traveling in a manner that may pose a threat. Another example is a pressure alarm system that causes a horn to blow and/or lights to flash if pressure is reaching critical limits in a vessel or tank. All readers should be familiar with the idiot lights in an automobile, which warn the driver of low oil pressure, open doors, and other potential problems.

In given situations, both extrinsic and intrinsic barriers may be used together. Devices may be designed to fail-safe if limits are exceeded or destruct in a fashion to minimize damage. Blowout pressure plugs on a process vessel are a prime example. Fuses and circuit breakers provide the same protection for electrical devices.

Administrative Barriers

The effects of threats can be minimized by administrative or soft barriers. The list of administrative barriers that can be put in place is limitless. Administrative barriers can take any form and most often are limited in their effectiveness by the failure of personnel to observe or implement them. Because of this fact, administrative and other soft barriers have the most potential for failure.

Examples of administrative barriers are work procedures (whether written or not), supervision, laws, codes, and standards. Each of these is intended to be a barrier to prevent a particular unwanted event from occurring. The problem with administrative barriers is that people sometimes do not do what they are supposed to do. For example, if personnel don't follow or otherwise circumvent the written procedure, they render the respective barrier ineffective.

In the irrigation example, training was provided and written procedures were in place to help ensure safe work practices. Supervision was considered adequate. Still, as evidenced by the event, procedures were not followed. It may have been that the written procedures were not understood, training was not effective, or supervision was not up to par.

Procedures and programs are only as effective as the personnel who implement them. That is why engineered solutions to produce physical barriers are generally preferred whenever possible. Engineered or hard solutions to the problem might include rerouting potentially interfering power lines, the use of nonconductive pipes, etc. Physical barriers are much harder to overlook.

Barrier Limitations

No matter how well thoughtout, designed, or implemented, barriers have limitations. They may not be practical or may not be implemented because they are not in line with management objectives. The technology to implement the proposed barrier may not be available yet or may not be economically feasible to implement. This is illustrated in the irrigation case.

The company responsible for power generation and distribution could have insulated the overhead power lines to prevent contact by unsuspecting field irrigators. Or, they could have elevated all power lines in the system high enough above ground level to avoid being hit by pipe, cranes, or other objects. However, neither of these solutions seem reasonable in an economic or practical sense.

Another consideration is that no matter how well thought out, barriers may simply fail partially or totally due to unforeseen circumstances. For example, law enforcement officers wear bulletproof vests for personal protection. This barrier, however, doesn't protect the officer's legs, arms, or head. If an officer were to be shot in the leg, he would be injured. This injury would not be the result of a barrier failing, as bulletproof vests are intended only to protect the trunk and not the legs. However, if during a conflict the straps of that vest are loosened, the vest falls off, and the officer is shot in the stomach, we could say that the barrier had failed.

If barriers are not used, their effectiveness is negated. In the case of the irrigator, there were both physical and administrative barriers in place. The power lines were at an acceptable level above ground to prevent *most* events from occurring, except for the unlikely event of someone wielding a 40-foot conductor. The farmer had specific procedures in place directing farm workers in the changing of irrigation handlines, training had been performed in a timely manner, and safety meetings were held regularly. In this case, personnel performance (specifically, poor work practices) was the root cause of the event. It might be said that the in-place barriers, mostly administrative, were less-than-adequate in preventing the event.

Structure of Barriers

Barriers can be installed in singular or multiple fashion. They can be placed around, between, or applied directly to either the target or the threat, to separate the two. Figures 9.1 through 9.8 display these concepts.

Figure 9.1 shows energy passing through a single barrier to affect a target. In this case, the barrier in place has been breached and would therefore be considered less than adequate.

Figure 9.2 illustrates an adequate barrier. The energy trace from the threat is successfully contained by the barrier and thereby prevented from reaching the target.

Figure 9.3 portrays the concept of multiple barriers. This also may be thought of as barrier redundancy. For example, during procurement activities, several barriers might be considered useful in preventing problems from occurring: design control, drawing control, procurement control including the pre-approval of vendors, training, etc.

Figure 9.1
Failure of Single Barrier

The following series of figures show how a barrier or series of barriers may be bypassed, ignored, or circumvented (Figure 9.4). An example would be that of personnel not following written work procedures. The barrier is in place, but it is not used; it is ignored or worked around. Another example would be the posted speed limit, intended to designate the normal safe speed for negotiating a curve in the road. To effectively deal with the situation that one barrier may be ignored or missed, it

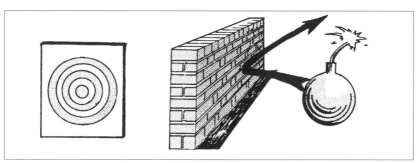

Figure 9.2
Effective Single Barrier

often is necessary to build additional controls into the system. These controls might include tightening procedures and strengthening personnel accountability for events that occur because of these actions. In the case of the speed limit, there may be a safety margin built in by the banking of the curve and speed limits in general checked by police action.

There is a theory that all barriers contain holes or ways in which they can be penetrated. Another way of stating this would be that barriers, by deliberate design or oversight, do not allow for all possible conditions in which the threat and target might come together. Provided this particular

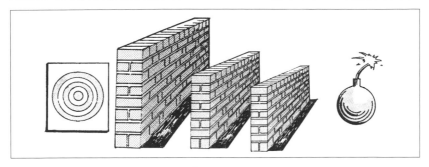

Figure 9.3
Multiple Barriers

condition does not occur, there is, of course, no problem. Even when barriers are installed in multiple fashion, these holes, which exist in each single barrier, allow a problem to occur if the holes line up, providing a clear path for the threat to reach the target. Figure 9.5 illustrates this concept.

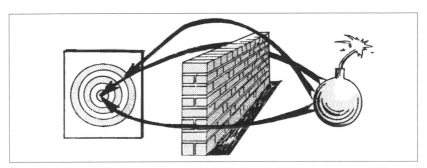

Figure 9.4
Bypassing of Barrier

When barriers are found to be inadequate, they may be strengthened to prevent passage through (or around) them. Figure 9.6 represents the concept of a strengthened barrier.

Figure 9.7 demonstrates a barrier completely surrounding a threat to contain unwanted energy flow. This is a preferred solution when possible. Examples of this type of totally enclosing barrier include pressure vessels and containment structures.

Figure 9.8 shows a barrier surrounding a target. This method is preferred when it is impractical or impossible to place adequate barriers around a threat. An example of this is illustrated in underwater hard-hat diving. In hard-hat diving the person is enclosed or surrounded by a protective suit made of a canvas type material and wears a metal hat with

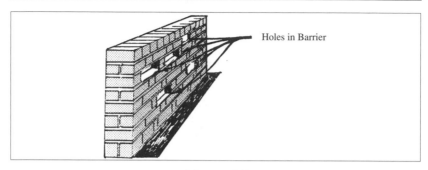

Figure 9.5
Holes in Barrier

air hoses connected to it. This places the person in an environment conducive to life and protects the diver from an otherwise threatening underwater environment. In this case it is easier to enclose the target than the threat.

Figure 9.9 displays the concept of surrounding barriers placed around *both* the threat and the target. To ensure safety in areas of high risk, it is best to consider barriers enclosing both the threat and the target. For example, consider a nuclear power plant and the people doing maintenance work in it. There are numerous design barriers that protect workers from exposure to radiation. These range from pressure and contain-

Figure 9.6
Strengthening Barriers

ment vessels to limiting switches. There also are barriers placed on the workers themselves. These include safety training, work procedures, and special protective clothing which is worn when working in designated radiation zones.

144

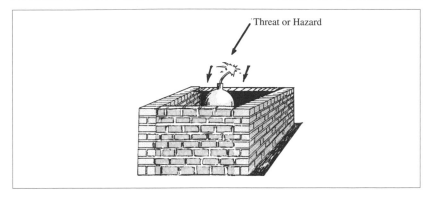

Figure 9.7
Complete Isolation Barrier

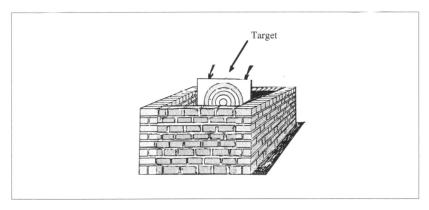

Figure 9.8
Isolating the Target

The Trace

Major undesired events or problems may result from a sequence, or chaining, of minor events. Taken by themselves, these individual events may not have much significance, but collectively they could produce an unwanted outcome since barriers are breached by the particular sequence of their occurrence. At other times, it is a singular trace (one event) which breaches any in-place barrier. It is necessary to trace the threat back to its origin and find the initial release of unwanted energy. During this process, the adequacy of existing barriers is determined.

In the irrigation case, it is easy to identify the final result. Events and conditions surrounding this accident seemed to be a normal part of everyday operations. Tracing back from the final event of Elmo

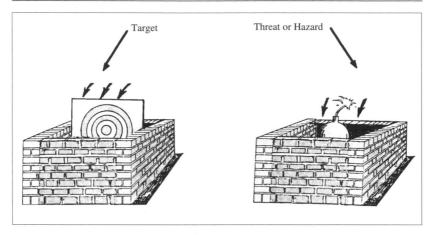

Figure 9.9
Isolating the Target and the Threat

coming in contact with the power lines, at least one physical (hard) and two administrative (soft) barriers have been breached. The hard barrier was the height of the power lines given the improbable event of an extremely long conductor (the pipe). One soft barrier was the work procedure, another was the safety training. The thing that caused these barriers to be breached was disregard of, or failure to follow, procedures; in this particular sequence, what we have called bad judgment.

You can postulate that another barrier was breached. More direct supervision might not have allowed Elmo to perform the task alone. Not stepping in to prevent Elmo's solo act was bad judgment on the part of the supervision (assuming he knew Elmo was working alone). You can examine the usual work practices and examine the routine that should have been followed when Elmo's helper didn't show up for work. This action in itself should not have caused any harm, but it does demonstrate that the buddy system effectiveness was limited by lack of adequate checks and balances.

Reactive Analysis Process

In the preceding sections of this chapter, the elements of barrier analysis were discussed. Targets, barriers, threats, and traces were examined. This next section explains how to perform a barrier analysis. We will describe completing the worksheet by columns. As was noted in Chapter 8, the worksheet may be completed in different fashion, i.e., line by line. The choice of approach usually is a matter of preference on the part of the analyst, since the completed worksheets are the same if done properly. Figure 9.10 shows a typical barrier analysis worksheet.

The first step in performing a barrier analysis to determine the root cause of an unwanted event or problem is to define those things of value or targets that have been damaged. Remember that as the result of a single event, many (related) damages can occur. It is good practice to list *all* potential targets initially, allowing the subsequent analysis to eliminate those not affected by the event. In the case of the irrigation worker, the accident caused severe injury to the worker. This is the most obvious and direct injury or damage and should be listed first. However, there may be adverse impacts on the supervisor, the person responsible for training, the farm operator or owner, and others.

Depending upon the magnitude of the problem, the possible harm to these (and other) targets may need to be analyzed. For purposes of development, only the direct injury to Elmo Fiero will be examined here.

The next step is to identify the source of the threat. In the example, the source of the threat was obviously the overhead power lines, more specifically the electrical energy which was diverted.

Once the target damage and threat have been identified, the next step is to identify any barriers that should have prevented the undesired event from occurring. The barriers in the case include procedures for changing handlines, safety training on the hazards of upending handlines in the vicinity of power lines, supervision, and the height of the power lines from ground level.

TARGET	THREAT	BARRIER	ANALYSIS

Figure 9.10
Typical Barrier Analysis Worksheet

Once all barriers have been identified, analyze their adequacy. Ask the question, "Were there barriers in place to minimize the effect of harmful contact with threats and, if so, were they adequate to prevent unwanted events from occurring?" All too often, when barriers fail, there is no backup. In analyzing an accident, examine any additional barriers to see if they were adequate to divert the threat from the target when any primary barrier was breached.

Other questions to ask include the following.

■ Were physical barriers placed on or surrounding the threat or potential hazard operational?

■ Was the barrier (or barriers) placed between the target and the source of the threat capable of handling the threat?

■ Were targets protected by working barriers?

■ Was it possible to protect the targets with barriers?

■ Were barriers backed up by contingency plans or other forms of administrative control?

Displayed in Figure 9.11 is an example of how you might show the targets, threats, and barriers in an analysis.

Most barriers include some assumed risk. If adequately designed, barriers include potential breaching scenarios to provide a reasonable risk zone. It is usually impractical to consider all possible accident scenarios, however unlikely, nor all possible ways that might be devised to thwart the barrier. The power company assumes some risk due to the final choice regarding the height of their power transmission lines. They could be higher, but in addition to cost and mechanical considerations, their own workers would be placed in greater jeopardy (more risk of

TARGET	THREAT	BARRIER	ANALYSIS
Elmo Fiero	Electricity	Height of power lines.	Usually adequate, but breached by conductive pipe.
		Work practices (buddy system).	Did not follow.

Figure 9.11
Partial Barrier Analysis—Elmo Fiero Accident

accidents) working on higher lines. The farm owner also assumes some risk by relying primarily on soft barriers, such as supervision and training. If the farm owner had recognized this type of accident as likely, nonconductive irrigation lines or underground distribution could be used. Of course, the worker assumes a risk by failing to follow procedures.

Each of the less-than-adequate barriers could be attributed to a different apparent cause. Often several failed barriers exhibit the same apparent cause; sometimes, although rarely, all failures can be attributed to the same cause. If several apparent causes are listed, the *one* root cause must be determined. As in mathematics the terms can be grouped and the constant (or common denominator) identified. In most analyses, however, the true root cause can be identified using either of the following logic techniques: the predominant cause, or the trigger cause.

The first technique utilizes the common thread logic approach, selecting as the root cause that of any of the listed causes which appears most often in explaining inadequate barriers. The pattern should be clear, the predominance readily apparent, and any cause/effect logic definable.

The second technique is the trigger analogy, identifying the cause that, if eliminated, would preclude the event from happening. This subtractive technique can allow that the others remain as identified, and the probability of occurrence of the event is significantly reduced, if not eliminated.

The trigger cause technique works particularly well in the case study. While written procedures might have been inadequate, training ineffective, direct supervision more clearly provided, and so on, the trigger event had to be the decision by Elmo to work alone. Experience alone should have been his guide. It is easy, but often wrong, to place the blame on the individual rather than the system. In cases such as this one, however, it is a proper call. In the case of the speeding violations, in spite of posted signs, the potential for police intervention, and other barriers, the individual must assume some, if not all, the fault when caught. It should not be interpreted from this assessment of blame that things cannot be improved. Additionally, the chances of such an event recurring cannot be minimized.

Recommendation for corrective and preventive action should be part of any analysis. In this case, workers should not be allowed in the field by themselves, but should have a spotter/helper with them to help change handlines when near overhead hazards. The system used to ensure this should be examined and strengthened if necessary. Another corrective action would be to consider another form of irrigation (e.g., underground lines), or eliminating the threat with nonconductive irrigation lines.

Prospective Barrier Analysis

In order to perform prospective barrier analysis to prevent unwanted events, four elements must be considered. First, an inventory of the things of value or targets that could be influenced by hazards should be listed (e.g. personnel, property, the company's reputation).

Secondly, potential sources of threats that could adversely impact these targets can be identified. It may be worthwhile to assign likelihoods of their occurrence at this point, if possible.

The third element is to examine any existing barriers and their adequacy in terms of keeping targets from coming into contact with threats or vice versa. Postulate scenarios in which the threats and targets could come into contact. If barriers do not exist, consider putting them in place if the probability of occurrence warrants this approach. Factors that should be considered were discussed in the section "Barriers."

Prospective barrier analysis should therefore consider factors related to controlling potential threats and targets, as well as the adequacy of barriers put into place to control or prevent events from occurring. Consideration should be given to factors that protect people, buildings, grounds, hardware, and production processes, as well as factors that relate to the reputation and liability of a company itself. Consideration also should be given to broader issues, such as goodwill, community, relationships, and corporate responsibility.

Summary

Barrier analysis can be an effective technique to identify the root cause of an unwanted event or problem. In addition to finding the cause of problems, barrier analysis techniques can be used in a prospective mode to examine the effectiveness of in-place measures (as well as identify others that may be needed) to prevent postulated events or incidents from occurring. Because of its focus on barriers or safeguards, it is extremely useful in programmatic or system analyses and certain types of accidents or events.

10

EVENTS AND CAUSAL
FACTORS ANALYSIS

"Nothing ever comes to pass without a cause."

—Philip Doddridge (1702-1751),

The Freedom of the Will

Introduction

Generally speaking and perhaps contrary to what some people might like to believe, things usually don't just "happen." In fact, there is considerable debate regarding "how things happened"; take, for example, the creation of the universe itself. Different schools of philosophy have widely diverging viewpoints on the subject of cause and effect, order vs. chaos, and so on. It is not our intention to explore this subject in detail, so the premise we will adopt is that an event, occurrence, problem, accident, etc., *is usually* traceable to some condition or previous event which was a direct or contributory cause. In terms of events and causal factors, this is stated: "For every accident, incident or problem, there was a previous or missed event or an underlying condition (or conditions) that caused it to happen."

Events and causal factors analysis examines events and conditions (and how these conditions influenced the events) by constructing and then examining the chronology or sequence of events and related conditions. The analysis is based on the premise that accidents, incidents or problems can be studied as the outcome or result of one or more successive events. Each of the events in the series being considered may be influenced by conditions, termed *causal factors*. These conditions or causal factors may be directly contributory, causal, or systemic in terms of the events being analyzed.

Quite often the investigator will discover that, taken by themselves, the sequence of events may not suggest the likely occurrence of an accident, incident, or problem. It is only when the circumstances surrounding the event (causal factors influencing these events) are considered that the seemingly innocuous sequence results in the event or problem.

This paradox sometimes requires that situational differences be identified first. (Regarding this, the reader may find some of the discussion in Chapter 8 useful.) In other cases, it may be necessary to examine why certain safeguards or barriers, intended to prevent or mitigate the event, failed to do so. This concept is discussed in Chapter 9.

As is the case with all the root cause analysis techniques discussed in this book, events and causal factors analysis may be used in a prospective mode. By carefully examining the (routine) sequence of operations or activities, potential problems may be noted. By planning and adding safeguards or controls at the appropriate points, or introducing changes to current operations or activities (thereby providing positive factors to influence these events), future problems may be mitigated or avoided altogether.

Introductory Story
The following story will be referred to throughout this chapter to help explain how to perform an events and causal factors analysis.

A vibration hammer was to be removed from a powder handling bag filter area. These vibration devices are used on solid handling operations to ensure against material buildup. This particular hammer was located on the fourth level of the processing plant.

Removal was to be accomplished by cutting the hammer's two angle iron supports using an oxyacetylene torch. Cutting metal in this fashion is fairly routine. Since high temperatures are developed, the procedure usually is monitored and controlled. In fact, company procedures required obtaining a welding and burning permit to ensure that adequate safeguards were considered. The cutting area was approximately two feet above a metal grating floor covered by rubber matting.

Two boilermakers, Alphonso and Bravuro O'Brien; a welder, Dan T. Inferno; and a plant operator, Olivia Smedley, were assigned to the task. A copy of the cutting permit was at the job location; however, the cutting permit had not been signed by the maintenance manager. The cutting permit required combustibles to be covered, but it did not specify the type of covering to be used. Olivia and Alphonso prepared the site by placing aluminum foil-backed Kraft paper around the immediate cutting area to cover the gap between the floor and the bag filter walls. As foil paper had been used for grinding operations in the past, they considered it to be sufficiently fire retardant.

The first angle iron support was cut off and removed without incident. Bravuro tended the oxygen and acetylene bottles while acting as a fire watch on the tower's second level. Alphonso assisted Dan (the welder) while Olivia acted as the fire watch on the fourth level. While removing the second bracket, molten drippings ignited the Kraft paper below the bracket. Alphonso attempted to smother the fire with a pair of spare coveralls which were lying nearby. Seconds later, however, the fire rekindled and Alphonso now attempted to put out the fire with a fire extinguisher which was hanging on a nearby wall. Since Alphonso was unfamiliar with how to activate the fire extinguisher, he assumed that it did not work. He then asked Olivia to get another nearby fire extinguisher. With her assistance, the second fire extinguisher was activated and the flame extinguished.

Olivia then noticed that the fire had damaged the vibrator power cord and went down to the third level to double check that the power had been turned off, as it should have been. When she got there, she spotted smoke and immediately went back up to the fourth level for a respirator mask. When she returned a few seconds later, the smoke was much thicker. She then instructed Bravuro on the level below to pull the fire alarm pull box and evacuate the building. After that, she returned upstairs to help Alphonso and Dan evacuate the building as well. Since the smoke on the lower floors was so thick, they went up to the roof, closing the fire door behind them. Once out on the building roof, Olivia radioed the plant manager for additional help.

The fire department responded quickly. Using self-contained breathing apparatus to enter the building, the firefighters promptly extinguished the fire. An investigation into the cause of the fire followed. Plant personnel were interviewed and the immediate scene of the fire was examined.

The fire department's investigation concluded that the probable source of the fire was a bag of cleaning rags left on the third level floor immediately below the cutting area. Most likely, hot slag from the cutting operation burned through the foil paper and fell onto the bag of rags below. The burning rags ignited the rubber matting on the third level floor, producing a great amount of black smoke. Burning rubber material fell through the third level grating and ignited two boxes of filters on the second level concrete floor.

Other Facts

It was discovered that none of the supervisory or required plant personnel (plant manager, maintenance personnel, craft supervisor, nor the safety engineer) had actually inspected the work location prior to the start of cutting. The cutting permit required the craft supervisor to inspect the job site for permit compliance and then sign off the back of the permit before cutting could begin.

Aluminum-backed Kraft paper was utilized as a fire-resistant blanket below the job site to prevent flame and hot material from dropping to the floor below, and to protect equipment in the immediate vicinity. This paper had been utilized in the past to protect equipment during grinding operations, but not welding operations. Both the safety engineer and craft supervisor later affirmed that this particular material would not have been allowed, had they been aware of its use.

Proper fire watch procedures require an observer to be on the level below the cutting operation, since the floor was on open metal grating. Because of a plant modernization process, this work was performed on a weekend to maintain schedule. The craft supervisor, aware that the work was under way, decided that it was relatively routine and the risk worth the shortcuts taken.

Needless to say, around the water coolers, the incident became known as "Dan T's inferno." Despite her lack of knowledge of fire-resistant material, Olivia was widely praised for her cool head during the incident. Alphonso and Bravuro, badly shaken by their experience, left the company shortly thereafter and became fire protection equipment salesmen.

We will use this story later in this chapter to demonstrate the use of events and causal factors analysis. But first, let's examine the basics of this technique.

Elements of Events and Causal Factors Analysis

As suggested by this section's title, there are two basic elements to events and causal factors analysis: the event sequence and causal factors or conditions that did (or might have) influenced or contributed to these events. This section will discuss these basic elements and develop the protocols for charting an events and causal factors diagram. It will describe the usual format for the events, causal factors (conditions), event sequences, and methods used to eventually identify the root cause.

Format

The basic format and conventions adopted in constructing an events and causal factors diagram (Figure 10.1) are described below. Although other symbols may be used, the following format and conventions are consistent with those contained in the Department of Energy's Accident/Incident

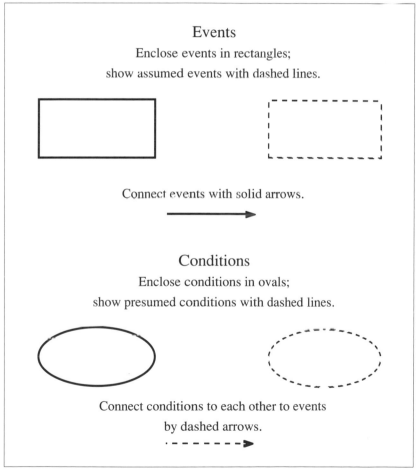

Events

Enclose events in rectangles;
show assumed events with dashed lines.

Connect events with solid arrows.

Conditions

Enclose conditions in ovals;
show presumed conditions with dashed lines.

Connect conditions to each other to events
by dashed arrows.

Figure 10.1
Symbols for Events and Causal Factors

Investigation Manual (DOE/SSDC 76-45/27, SSDC 27, Second Edition) and also those used extensively throughout the nuclear power industry.

The first item to be discussed is the graphical presentation of the two constituent items: events and causal factors. More specific discussion for both events and conditions (causal factors) is provided in this chapter's sections "Criteria for Event Descriptions" and "Criteria for Condition Descriptions."

1. Enclose events in rectangles; enclose conditions in ovals. Each event and condition which is based on valid observation or factual evidence is drawn with solid borders; assumed events or conditions should be clearly identified as such by dashed line rectangles and ovals. The latter (assumed events and conditions) usually are included on the diagram as needed to visualize the process; however, since they are not based on facts, their use should be limited. Assumed events and conditions can be fertile breeding ground for serious errors and bias during the analysis.

2. Arrange events chronologically from left to right (the usual progression for a time series).

3. Show the events in their actual sequence; do not make assumptions since the problem may later be determined by the fact that an operation or activity was, in fact, performed out of sequence and this materially affected the results. Show any related pre-events, the event (problem, accident, incident itself), and the post-event or amelioration phase. Include only pertinent events or occurrences in this sequence. The beginning and end of the event sequence will need to be established (advice on this aspect is provided later in the chapter).

Analysts frequently start with the actual problem or incident as the middle event and then proceed in both directions to reconstruct both the pre- and post-events.

4. Connect all events by solid arrows.

5. Connect conditions to each other and to related events by dashed arrows. Figure 10.2 shows what a basic events and causal factors diagram looks like.

6. If necessary, depict secondary event sequences, contributing factors, and systemic factors using horizontal lines at different levels below the primary sequence (see Figure 10.3).

We have begun our explanation of events and causal factors analysis by first telling you how the diagram is constructed. Events and causal factors analysis is a highly visual technique, providing a story line (event sequence) with accompanying explanations or descriptions of conditions surrounding these events (causal factors).

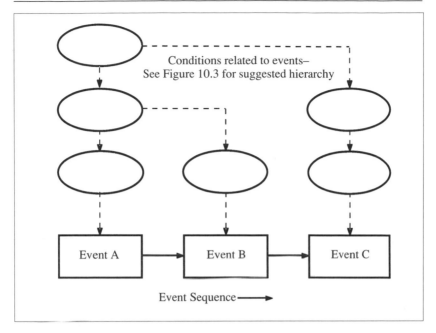

Figure 10.2
Basic Events and Causal Factors Chart

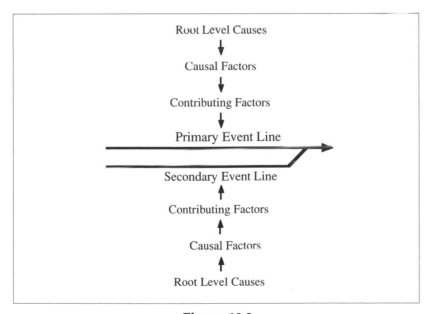

Figure 10.3
Primary and Secondary Events and Causal Factors

To ensure that the two elements which comprise the diagram are utilized properly, the following discussion regarding criteria for events and conditions is provided. To more clearly demonstrate these ideas, refer to the introductory story throughout this chapter.

Criteria for Event Descriptions

1. An event is an occurrence or happening. It should not describe a condition, state, circumstance, issue, conclusion, or result. For example, one of the events in the introductory story, when correctly stated, is "Kraft paper caught on fire." An improper event statement (since it is an opinion or conclusion) would be "Kraft paper was inadequate"; this statement is, in fact, a condition or explanatory factor.

2. Each event should be shown on the diagram as a rectangle which contains a short sentence with one subject and one active verb. It is best to describe each event separately. For example, one event from the story is "Kraft paper caught on fire." When several separate events are described together, such as "Kraft paper caught fire and was extinguished," it may cause the subsequent analysis to miss potentially important intervening events or factors which should be considered; for example, the ineffective attempt to smother the fire with coveralls, as well as the difficulties Alphonso had in operating the first fire extinguisher.

3. Each event should be as precisely stated as possible. This certainly will be of value in the subsequent analysis. Overlooked facts may emerge in rereading the event description. For example, "Alphonso attempted to smother the fire with coveralls" would be preferable to "Alphonso attempted to put out the fire," since it is more definitive.

4. Each event should be quantified to the extent possible; i.e., "the fire spread to two floors," not "the fire spread."

5. If possible, each event should include time and date. Sometimes there are important clues embedded in elapsed times or in the particular date, day, or time.

6. Show the events in their actual sequence. Then check this actual sequence against that which is normal or logical. There may be an indication that one or more steps in the sequence have been omitted. If this performance of activities or operations in the order shown would likely cause a problem, then the analysis process is greatly simplified.

Event Sequence/Relationship

The event sequence should depict the pre-event, event, and post-events in their chronological order to provide a clear picture of what happened.

Remember that one of the advantages of the technique is this visual representation of the sequence of events. Look at the representation with the eyes of an eventual reader. Make sure it is accurate and understandable. If it is necessary to show how two entirely separate sequences of events came together to cause the event or problem, use primary and secondary sequence lines. The primary and secondary events lines should be constructed as shown in Figure 10.3.

In addition to readability, the chain of events must be reviewed for clarity and correctness, since the sequence forms the eventual baseline of the subsequent root cause analysis.

A practical suggestion: When constructing the events line, first list *every* event which is part of the sequence (story element) using a worksheet similar to that shown in Figure 10.4. Then determine which of these events apply to the problem at hand. Use the simple headings "yes," "no," and "not sure." Include only the "yes" and "not sure" events in the initial events line. This will aid in paring down the diagram to include only those events pertinent to the problem. Further discussion of this technique is included in the section "Collecting and Arranging the Events Chronologically."

Criteria for Condition Descriptions

The criteria for describing conditions are similar to those given above. Conditions or causal factors should 1) be precisely described, 2) be quantified whenever possible, 3) be posted with time and date, when possible, and 4) logically proceed from the event in the hierarchy shown in Figure 10.3 (direct or contributory, then causal, and then generic or root cause).

Event	Pertinent to Problem?		
	Yes	No	Not Sure
1.			
2.			
3.			
4.			

Figure 10.4
Preliminary Events List

Conditions are different from events. They describe circumstances or states, as opposed to occurrences or happenings. Conditions are therefore passive rather than active, describing states or circumstances. For example, a condition description based on the introductory story already discussed is "Kraft paper not adequate."

There will be a tendency when defining conditions or causal factors to introduce the analyst's beliefs into the process. Potential bias will be a problem, unless all the logic rules stated herein are followed. In each case, examine the cause and effect relationship stated. "Kraft paper not adequate for this use" (cause) relates directly to "Kraft paper catches fire" (event), given the preceding event "Hot slag falls on Kraft paper." In another situation, this cause may not fit; "Kraft paper was not adequate," for example, may not make sense if it really did not contribute to the eventual problem or event. Remember that foil-backed Kraft paper seemed adequate for protection during grinding operations, where there are also hot particles dropping.

Process of Events
and Causal Factors Analysis

Events and causal factors analysis can be defined as a series of the following seven steps:
- Collecting and arranging the events chronologically
- Defining the event of interest
- Selecting the scope of analysis
- Examining the event sequence for problems
- Defining and relating contributing conditions to each event
- Continuing to define causal factors and root level or systemic causes
- Determining the root cause

Each of these steps is discussed in further detail below. The process of testing the sequence and the relationship of causal factors is an important part of the process. In fact, this continual "testing" process is pervasive and applies to all of the other steps listed above. The relationship of cause and effect which forms the basis of the technique may also be the source of its most serious problems. An improper cause and effect relationship may affect not only that particular portion of the analysis but the overall results as well.

Collecting and Arranging the Events Chronologically
The first step in events and causal factors analysis is to determine all pertinent events and arrange them in chronological fashion. This becomes

the eventual story line. This process is greatly simplified if the advice given earlier is followed regarding the selection and inclusion of only those events which relate to the problem at hand.

Events should be arranged in chronological order from left to right, starting with pre-events, the event of interest (discussed below), followed by any post-event events and actions necessary to understand the story. Known events should be enclosed in solid rectangles. When an event is assumed to have taken place or is inferred from the logical progression, it should be enclosed in a rectangle using dashed lines. (Refer to Figure 10.1.) This distinction between actual and presumed events will be important when the sequence is examined later.

The sequence also may be determined using the testimony of witnesses. It usually is good practice to involve only those with firsthand knowledge of the event; event sequences; or the condition of people, places, or things relevant to the event or problem. It is also good practice to remember that eyewitnesses to an event may perceive the same situation quite differently; any trained accident investigator can testify to this fact. Remember the story of the "drunk" driver in Chapter 8. When substantial differences are noted, it is worthwhile to try to resolve them before considerable time has elapsed. People's memories are perhaps the most volatile evidence that can be obtained. It is useful to take photographs and obtain samples or other hard evidence if possible.

A practical suggestion: When constructing an events and causal factors chart, write both the events and conditions (discussed later) on Post-it™ notes. This will give you greater flexibility to rearrange the events and conditions as you proceed with the analysis of the event or problem.

The next step is to connect the events on the diagram by solid arrows. As indicated above, each event should either be based upon valid factual evidence or be clearly indicated as presumptive by dashed lines. The primary sequence of events is depicted as a straight horizontal line. If needed, secondary event sequences should be depicted on a second horizontal line below the primary event sequence. (The reader is again referred to Figures 10.2 and 10.3.)

The complexity of the event or problem will suggest both the need for and detail of any coding to be applied. Coding may be necessary for particularly lengthy, complex, or elaborate diagrams. When applied, coding facilitates understanding the charted display and also serves to reference supporting documentation, detailed descriptions, or observations. Events can be coded in any fashion useful to the reader or analyst, such as numerically (1-n.xx) or alphabetically (A-Z.xx).

Defining the Event of Interest

One of the most important aspects of an events and causal factors analysis is defining the event of interest in the overall sequence. This is important because the event immediately preceding this event of interest usually gives the analyst the real jumping off point for the evaluation. For example, in our story, it would be tempting to say the fire was the event of interest. The fire was only a predictable result of flammable material from hot drippings resulting from the cutting operation. The real question is how these hot drippings fell to the material or why, given this circumstance, the material was not suitably fireproof.

For example, an analyst might be investigating a nuclear reactor scram. (A scram is an automatic shutdown of the reactor for any number of reasons.) Let us assume in this particular case the scram occurred because of high flux values. The scram is an automatic response to the high flux condition; there is practically no insight to be gained here. The scram itself is what is supposed to happen; the real question is: What caused the high flux condition that in turn precipitated the scram?

Experienced analysts use this technique, focusing on the event or events immediately preceding the accident or problem. Once the event of interest has been identified, then a more detailed analysis, perhaps using change or barrier analysis of the initiating events, will reveal the problem cause.

Selecting the Scope of Analysis

The next step is determining the overall scope of the analysis. The scope should be limited to those events and conditions that are relevant to the event or problem itself. It is unnecessary to extend the analysis beyond what is needed to accurately depict the event situation. For example, in our introductory story you only need to trace the pre-events to that point in time that the primary event sequence makes sense. The most logical starting point is when the work assignment was made. In like fashion, the event sequence probably does not need to proceed much past the fire being extinguished and investigated by the fire department. By using the original work assignment as the starting point and the fire department's investigation as the closing event, the "story" has been adequately told. Actions taken as a result of the accident are better handled as a separate discussion of corrective, preventive or adaptive actions, and thereby not confused with the problem discussion.

Constructing the Diagram

To illustrate constructing an events and causal factors diagram, we will use the introductory story. The reader may wish to reread the story and make a list to compare with the following. Some of the pre-events were:

- Personnel assigned to the task
- Cutting permit obtained
- Olivia prepared site
- Kraft-backed paper placed as protection
- Bravuro attended oxygen and acetylene bottles
- Alphonso assisted Dan, the welder
- Olivia acted as fire watch
- Dan cut first angle iron
- First bracket removed
- Dan cut second angle iron

The accident or event situation in the story was, of course, the ensuing fire in the plant's powder handling building. The sequence of these events is as follows:

- Molten drippings ignite Kraft paper
- Alphonso attempted to smother fire
- Fire rekindled
- Vibrator cord damage noticed
- Alphonso tried to use fire extinguisher
- Alphonso then used another fire extinguisher
- Flames were extinguished
- Olivia went to third floor
- Olivia unplugged vibrator
- Olivia spotted smoke
- Olivia exited to get mask
- Olivia returned
- Smoke worsened
- Olivia told Bravuro to pull fire alarm
- Bravuro pulled fire alarm
- Bravuro evacuated building
- Olivia went back upstairs
- Olivia assisted Alphonso and Dan to roof

Post-events included:

- Olivia and Dan went upstairs to roof
- Olivia radioed plant manager
- Plant manager called fire department
- Power to the building was shut off
- Fire department arrived
- Fire department extinguished fire

The reader should note the detail provided in each of the event descriptions. Remember the advice provided earlier was to construct the original diagram with as much detail as possible, condensing events later, if desired, in the final version.

Examining the Sequence for Problems

It is sometimes possible to determine the cause of the problem by careful examination of the event sequence itself. Carefully examine any events depicted by dashed lines; determine their importance in terms of having occurred. Quite often, activities performed out of sequence or a missing or misperformed action will be the obvious cause of the event or problem. If this is the case, the analysis may be greatly simplified.

Sometimes this examination of the event sequence will raise questions warranting subsequent consideration and evaluation. In our story, considerable time and effort was expended in fighting the fire before the alarm was pulled. This is contrary to advice usually given by firefighting and safety professionals. It may be worthwhile to make a note to re-examine training and any instructions given on this subject later. This is another example of the positive outcomes, i.e., the identification of opportunities for improvement, that can accrue from root cause analysis of a problem.

Defining and Relating Contributing Conditions to Each Event

The next step is to define and relate the direct, contributing conditions surrounding or influencing each of the events. Conditions are depicted as ovals and connected to the event by dashed arrows. An example of a first level, direct contributory condition related to the event "Alphonso tried to use fire extinguisher" would be "Alphonso unfamiliar with its operation." This helps explain the unsuccessful event.

Known conditions or causal factors should be depicted as solid ovals, with assumed factors shown by dashed lines. In the example above, the condition would be shown as a solid oval, since the story states that Alphonso did not know how to operate the extinguisher. Had this not been given, there could be another explanation: the extinguisher was empty or discharged.

Readers are reminded again of the dangers in properly defining cause and effect relationships. It can be seen that the analysis could proceed entirely in a wrong direction, given just this difference in the reason an event occurred (or did not).

From the introductory story, other examples of direct contributory conditions are given:

- Improper fire retardant material used (goes with Kraft paper catches fire)
- Cutting permit did not specify proper material and conditions (goes with cutting permit obtained)
- Supervision less than adequate (starts with original personnel assignment)

Continuing to Define
Causal Factors and Root Level or Systemic Causes

To the extent possible, all direct, contributory conditions should be identified. The process continues by asking the "why" for each condition. For example, in the story, Alphonso did not understand the operation of the first fire extinguisher he tried. The delay was part of the sequence of events and had the fire been promptly extinguished, the fire might not have spread.

The next question (going to the causal factor) is "why?" Why didn't Alphonso know how to use the extinguisher? One answer is that training might be less than adequate, but examination of the causes listed in Chapter 3 reveals that it might not be Alphonso's training that was the cause, if it is subsequently discovered that he was never sent to any such training. If this were the case, it would be more appropriate to assign "planning," part of "management methods," as the apparent cause.

The preferred approach would then be to either assign "training less than adequate" as the apparent cause with a question mark or asterisk following this assignment to indicate the need to "check this later" or to assign both causes during the preliminary analysis. In any case, more facts will be needed to make a final determination of this apparent cause.

Determining the Root Cause

The events and causal factors diagram, properly constructed, eventually will yield the root cause. Refer again to Figures 10.2 and 10.3. As the conditions and causal factors are carried out far enough, the root cause eventually is reached. The analyst must continue to ask "why," progressing from the immediate and contributory factors through the more basic systemic and causal factors to the root cause level.

For example, consider the chain of conditions related to the event "Kraft paper placed as protection." The first-level condition might be "Kraft paper less-than-adequate for this use." Asking the next "why" gives a more basic reason,"Work permit not reviewed and approved." Although it might be presumed that the review of work permits would have detected the problem, asking the "why" to this second-tier condition gives an even more basic answer, "Lack of planning." This third and more basic factor can be attributed to management methods (see the root cause code listing in Chapter 3).

Management and supervision inadequacies become increasingly evident as all the less-than-adequate conditions are eventually brought to the rootcause level. It is obvious that the required planning and control of the activity was absent. The work was performed over a weekend to allow that schedules be met. It would be extremely unfair to blame the individuals for what happened, although often this is done. In this case, management abrogated its responsibilities and an unfortunate event resulted.

So, the final root cause for the accident in our story is management methods, specifically those aspects of planning and control of activities. Interestingly enough, there *were* procedures in place that might have prevented the occurrence; they were simply not followed. Failure to follow procedures can often be laid at the doorstep of individuals, but the lack of supervision and tacit management overlooking of requirements to meet schedule is far more obvious in this case. Workers are quick to pick up management and supervision's view of the rules.

Further Thoughts

The completed events and causal factors diagram should show all pertinent events and conditions. This diagram aids problem or event investigations by providing the event data organized in an understandable fashion. Analysis of the event sequence itself often helps to guide the investigation and identify missing or unclear events. Charting also helps to validate and confirm the true or actual event sequence. Events not in their proper position in the sequence or misperformed may suggest the problem's cause.

Events and causal factors analysis identifies and validates factual findings, probable causes, and contributing factors. It can help weigh and validate the accuracy of information from other analysis techniques.

The finished chart simplifies the organization of the investigation report. By graphically displaying pre-event, event, and post-event events and conditions, it is easier to identify primary and secondary events and conditions. Charting provides a greater understanding of how the problem occurred by illustrating the events, their sequence, and any associated conditions in an easy to understand format.

Process of Prospective
Events and Causal Factors Analysis

As with all the other root cause analysis techniques discussed in this book, events and causal factors analysis may be used in a prospective or forward-looking mode. The same techniques used to analyze problems or events also may be used to prevent or mitigate them. It remains a certainty that root cause analysis techniques have their greatest value when used to prevent problems, rather than solve them after they have occurred.

When used in a prospective mode, events and causal factors analysis can be used to ask questions such as:

- How can a sequence of events be constructed or predicted to ensure a particular outcome?
- Which conditions need to be present or controlled to cause the desired events to occur?
- Given a desired outcome based on a particular sequence of events and needed conditions to accomplish this, what intervening events or conditions might be necessary to achieve this?

All identified events and conditions need to be examined to determine if less than adequate conditions or the changes in the planned sequence of events may not result in the desired outcome. This may sound simple or obvious, but it is not always easy to do. Often events which inadvertently occur together, even seemingly innocuous when considered by themselves, could affect the desired outcome.

Events and causal factors analysis can also be used to postulate accident or incident sequences based on the current state of barriers and controls, sources of threats, environmental factors, and system dynamics. This technique is basically that used for war and management games.

Summary

Events and causal factors analysis provides a detailed analysis of the event sequence and associated causes or conditions. Events and causal factors charting is a very effective tool for analyzing why an event happened. The chronological layout of the event gives a complete and understandable picture of the entire event from pre-event conditions and circumstances through post-events.

Some key ideas to remember are:

- Events and causal factors analysis is a basic tool to depict, in logical sequence, the events and associated causal factors related to the occurrence of an event or problem.
- Events and causal factors analysis, while normally used for event investigation, can help validate the effectiveness of systems designed to prevent event occurrences.

Basic elements of events and causal factors analysis include:
- Events
- Sequence
- Conditions and causal factors
- Their relationship
- Identification of less-than-adequate items or conditions

Key steps in events and causal factors analysis are:
- Collect and arrange events chronologically
- Define the event of interest
- Select the scope of analysis
- Examine sequence for problems
- Define and relate conditions to events
- Define causal factors and root cause

As might be expected, events and causal factors analyses for extremely complicated events or problems can be quite elaborate and detailed. Even the events and causal factors diagram for the introductory story would be quite complex. Nonetheless, the chart can be quite useful in unravelling the chain of events.

Events and causal factors analyses often are used in conjunction with other root cause analysis techniques, particularly change and barrier analysis. Readers who are interested in furthering their skills in developing events and causal factors diagrams are referred to the case study provided in the accompanying workbook.

11

TREE DIAGRAMS

Introduction

When investigating events, it is sometimes difficult to visualize how a number of potential contributory factors could have caused the event. In the previous chapter, the events and related contributory factors were depicted using a straight line; sometimes a second line was added to show a parallel set of events and factors that impacted or influenced the primary or main sequence. When there are many factors involved and their relationship may also be important, tree diagrams are a better analysis technique to use.

A tree diagram is a graphical display of an event which logically describes each of the event's contributing factors. As the name implies, they look like trees (purists will argue that they only look like trees when they are upended).

Tree diagrams are extremely useful in helping visualize and analyze more complex systems or problem situations. Tree diagrams can be used as either reactive or prospective analysis tools. When used reactively to investigate accidents and events, they are called *fault* or *root cause trees*. Tree diagrams may also be used prospectively to systematically plan and organize requirements for organizations, programs and projects, or future improvements to current plant operations. Used for goal attainment, they are called *positive trees*. Tree diagrams can also be used to analyze the probability of an event happening; used in this fashion, they are termed *risk* or *probability trees.*

Introductory Story

The following case story will be referred to throughout the remainder of this chapter to help explain some of tree diagrams' concepts.

Elias Shamboch was a diligent employee. During his 15 years of service, he had never called in sick nor been late to work. He started as an apprentice welder and worked his way up the corporate ladder to his current position as vice president of operations. One of his responsibilities was to chair accident investigation boards if the need arose. To date, this had been a fairly rare occurrence. Today was different.

A longtime employee of the maintenance shop, Pettigrew Frondus, had been severely injured while working on a gravel-hauling trailer. During a routine welding operation, the gates that open and close at the trailer bottom accidentally closed on Pettigrew as he was attempting to enter through the bottom of the trailer to perform welding.

Elias Shamboch had investigated accidents before, but none of them had ever involved a close friend. He and Frondus started working for the company the same day. Over the years, they had formed a friendship. Pettigrew often referred to Elias as his "buddy up in the front office." In turn, Elias called Pettigrew "a burned out old welder."

After talking with maintenance personnel, Elias discovered that working conditions in the maintenance shop had become an issue over the past six months and many employees were complaining about unsafe procedures as well as being overworked. Both the day and night shifts were putting in a lot of overtime due to an increased demand for maintenance work.

While investigating the accident, Elias also discovered that no written procedures were in place to cover the particular welding task that Pettigrew Frondus had been performing. However, the following informal procedures were followed fairly consistently by all who performed the task:

- The belly dump trailer was backed over one of two pits to enable a person to stand up when welding instead of having to crawl under it to work.
- The emergency brakes on the truck and the trailer were set and the wheels were then blocked.
- The belly dump gates were opened and a temporary support bar was welded in place to keep the gates from closing inadvertently. The gates worked on air pressure. If the air pressure dropped below a certain level, the doors would close automatically. This ensured that no gravel

could escape should the trailer ever suddenly lose air pressure while moving down the highway.

■ The wear edges around the gate opening were welded with a hard surfacing weld rod to prevent the gravel from eventually wearing down the gates.

■ After completing the weld, the gate's air pressure was built up and the gates were switched to the open position. The temporary support bar was then knocked out with a sledgehammer.

Other information Elias discovered during the investigation included the following:

■ Neither of the regular maintenance bays were used. Instead, a maintenance bay without a stand-up pit was used.

■ This particular job was on a tight schedule. Downtime cost for the belly dump trailer was approximately $1,500 a day. There was, therefore, a lot of pressure to put the trailer back into operation.

■ Frondus, the accident victim, was working his 15th consecutive 14-hour shift.

■ Instead of welding the usual metal bar in place, a wooden 2 x 4 was used to keep the gates open.

■ The electric switch to activate the gate was not working. It had been jumpered with alligator clips.

■ The trailer's wheels were not blocked.

It takes an average of less than 1 second for the belly dump gates to close once either the switch is closed or there is a loss of air pressure

Elias shook his head as he returned to his office. The whole set of circumstances suggested an accident just waiting to happen. In fact, any one of these factors might have been enough to cause the accident to happen. He also wondered how many other operations might be like this. For the first time in years, he left work early that day. He went to the hospital to visit his old friend, Pettigrew.

Symbols Used in Tree Analysis

Before we proceed further, the symbols used in constructing tree diagrams will be provided. Rectangles, logic gates, and transfers are the basic symbols most often used in constructing tree diagrams. These symbols are shown and described below. Although the rectangle, triangle, and "AND" or "OR" logic gates are the only symbols most individuals will need or use to construct tree diagrams, other symbols will be presented. In addition, as an aid in maintaining the readability of a particularly large or complex tree diagram, a suggested numbering system for its components also is provided.

Rectangle

Rectangle: A rectangle is used to depict events, factors, or elements in a tree diagram. The use of a rectangle is consistent with their use in events and causal factors analysis. Generally speaking, as with other analysis techniques, it is better to list as many factors as possible during the initial tree construction. During the subsequent validation and analysis phases, certain events or elements may be combined or eliminated; however, doing this first may obscure the analysis or result in an important piece of the puzzle being overlooked.

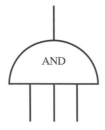

AND

"AND" Gate: AND and OR logic symbols are used to show how the various events, factors, or elements are considered when combining and analyzing them. An AND symbol denotes a particular logic as to how an output (subsequent event) occurs when two or more contributory events, factors, or elements are present or occur. The logic of the AND operator is the condition is "true" or can occur only when *all* input events occur or are present. It follows that, if any input is missing or does not occur, nothing happens. The symbol itself usually contains the identifying word "AND."

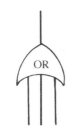

OR

"OR" Gate: The logical OR statement implies that a subsequent event will occur when one, several, *or* all of the contributory events, factors, or elements occur or are present. This logic is different than the AND statement, in which the event occurs only when *all* preceding events or conditions are present or occur. The logic symbol usually contains the identifying word "OR."

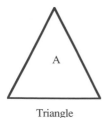

A

Triangle

Triangle: Quite often in the construction of larger trees, entire sections will be repeated in different locations. Alternatively, it may be desirable to construct a smaller subtree elsewhere to clearly define a certain (sub)set of particular interest. A triangle can be used to designate this connection or continuation. The triangle usually contains a letter as reference to the subtree's location as well as its fit on the main tree and vice versa.

The above symbols constitute those most often needed to construct tree diagrams. Other symbols that might be of some value in certain situations follow.

Constraint: A symbol used to describe conditions or constraints to a logic gate or event. The explanation or description is usually contained inside the ellipse. The reader is reminded of the similar use of this symbol in events and causal factors analysis. The meaning and use is the same here. While not suggesting their overuse in a tree diagram, constraints and conditions surrounding an event or element can help add insight to the analysis and subsequently to the reader.

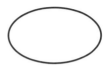

Ellipse

Scroll: A normally expected event that should have occurred during usual system operation. The use of this symbol is similar to the dashed line rectangle described in events and causal factors analysis. During the validation process described later, if a scroll appears in a path of interest, it should be verified as having taken place and, if so, changed to a rectangle. As with other analysis techniques, the analysis should not proceed with postulated or assumed events.

Scroll

Stretched Circle: A satisfactory event on a logic gate output. It is used to show completion of various portions of the analysis. This symbol indicates that the analysis need proceed no further on this particular branch.

Stretched Circle

Diamond: An undeveloped terminal event whose cause is not determined. It is terminated for lack of information or resources, or to avoid analysis redundancy. These symbols, by their very definition, truncate the development of that particular branch of the tree diagram.

Diamond

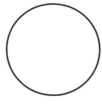

Circle: A base event requiring no further development. It is an independent event and usually is included to help readers' understanding of the problem or situation.

Circle

The reader is once again reminded that, aside from the first four or five symbols, these other symbols are not used regularly. However, it is good to know what they are and what they represent in case you want to do a fancy tree diagram for the front office. Chances are most people will not know what they are either; using these symbols gives you a chance to impress them. Needless to say, if they are used, their meaning should be provided in a "key" section on the tree diagram.

Numbering System: In the case of larger, more complex tree diagrams, it is helpful to number the events on the tree. This aids in referencing tree sections and may also be used to number supporting documentation, analysis portions, etc. A simple format can be used to number the events, such as a consecutive or tiered decimal system (described below).

Top Event
1.1 First Tier = First event on first tier.
2.1 Second Tier = First event on second tier.
3.1 Third Tier = First event on third tier.
3.2 Third Tier = Second event on third tier.

This particular numbering system is displayed in Figure 11.1.

A similar system can be used, if needed, to number events below a transfer symbol (triangle). The numbers should begin with the transfer symbol's alphabetic designator. This system of alphanumeric progression is shown below:

Alphanumeric Event Location
D   Transfer "D"
D.1.1   First subtier of transfer "D," first event.
D.2.1   Second subtier of transfer "D," first event.
D.2.2   Second subtier of transfer "D," second event.

An example of this type of transfer numbering system is displayed in Figure 11.2.

It should be pointed out that the purpose of describing additional symbols and suggesting numbering systems was to aid the analyst (and the subsequent readers) of the completed tree in describing the event or problem situation. To the extent that they are useful, they should be utilized. Usually they are not needed for smaller, simple tree diagrams.

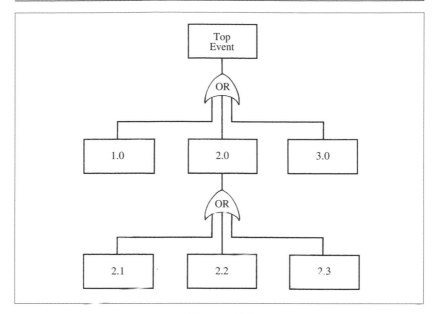

Figure 11.1
Suggested Numbering Scheme

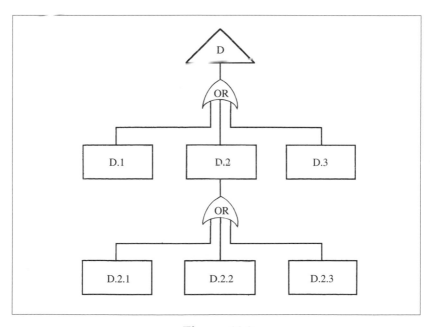

Figure 11.2
Transfer Numbering System

What is primarily important, of course, is not the readability of the completed tree diagram, but its truth or accuracy. An elegantly prepared tree diagram that is totally off the mark defeats its intended purpose.

Process of Reactive
or Root Cause Tree Analysis

The initial development of fault tree analysis is generally attributed to H. A. Watson of Bell Laboratories. Fault or root cause trees are usually constructed to analyze more complex problems or unwanted events and conditions. The Department of Energy (DOE) and the commercial nuclear industry routinely use fault or root cause tree analyses to investigate incidents and accidents, as well as to analyze equipment and safety system failures. The Management Oversight and Risk Tree (MORT—see Chapter 12) is a tree diagram particularly useful in the investigation of major accidents or serious injuries.

The process of constructing a tree diagram is relatively straightforward. Once the initial tree diagram has been constructed, it is then checked (verified) by reviewing its logic and relationships. This validation process, consisting of tracing each path through the tree, reveals oversights or faulty construction.

Once the tree has been constructed and validated, it is used to analyze the event or problem by postulating scenarios, selecting the most likely, and determining the root cause. This overall process will be described step by step in the following sections. To aid in understanding the construction and analysis of tree diagrams, elements of the introductory story will be introduced.

Defining the Top Event or Loss (Subject)
The first step in root cause tree analysis is to define the top event or loss. Simply stated, the top event is the subject of the analysis: lost performance, injuries, damage, loss of business, client or public support, or goodwill, etc. In the introductory story, the top event or subject of the resultant tree diagram would be the injury to Pettigrew Frondus, the maintenance worker. There is some strategy involved in selecting the subject. Since we have chosen Pettigrew's injury as the top event or subject of the tree, when the analysis is completed, we should then remember to look sideways at the potential for other injuries to other workers in other situations. Remember that preventing recurrence and systematic improvement should be the focus of all root cause efforts.

On the other hand, if we had chosen the (broader) subject of potential (including, of course, actual) worker injuries, then the focus of the subsequent analysis might have to be narrowed during the conclusion to adequately address the specific accident. There is no advice as to which approach might be better; they are both appropriate when properly developed. The only caution necessary is that the analyst remain aware of the inquiry's scope.

Constructing the Tree

Construction of the initial tree diagram continues with the listing of major contributory factors under the top event. The first level under the top event *usually* consists of the following factors:

- Personnel
- Material or equipment
- Procedures
- Other (optional)

The reader is referred to the chart of root causes in Chapter 3 as the source of these basic factors or problem elements. These major factors are shown on the left-hand side of the root cause chart and represent the grouping of several other, more specific root causes. Those involved in the service industries may wish to substitute "items/services" for "material or equipment."

To illustrate the progress so far, Figure 11.3 shows the construction of our basic tree diagram with three of the second tier factors suggested

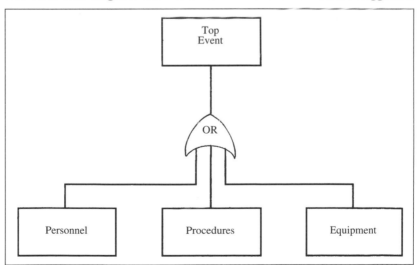

Figure 11.3
Partial Tree Diagram

above: personnel, procedures and material, or equipment (the optional "other" category was not included).

Continue Branching

The construction of the tree continues by the branching process. To add the next (third) level to the fault tree, further, specific items will be listed under each of the second level factors of personnel, material or equipment, and procedures. For example, under "procedures," the next level of detail might include:

■ Procedures not available
■ Procedures not up-to-date
■ Procedures not accurate or reviewed
■ Procedures not understandable or clear
■ Procedure not workable

Similarly, under the second-level factor of "equipment or material," further breakdown might be provided as follows:

■ Design less than adequate
■ Improper material selection
■ Improper manufacture
■ Improper installation
■ Improper maintenance
■ Improper operation
■ Improper storage

Returning to the example, there were many factors involved in the introductory story which might have contributed to the accident. These included: procedures used in the work process or activity (whether written or not); materials used in the task itself or as safety devices; training and experience of personnel assigned to the task; supervision; management; and the work environment.

The next step is to add these third-level items to the tree under each of the appropriate second-level descriptors. (The reader may wish to refer to Figure 3.4 again as well as the accompanying discussion of causal factors to gain better understanding of this process.) Organizing these factors in the logical groupings shown facilitates subsequent analysis efforts. There is a logic to this process and an analyst will get better at constructing trees that are initially complete and accurate as he/she constructs more trees. It's as much an art as a science.

Some of the elements from the story are shown under each of the appropriate second level factors in Figure 11.4.

Although we will not develop this tree further, it should be pointed out that this tree could be branched further if necessary. Another (fourth) level could be added to provide further detail under each of the

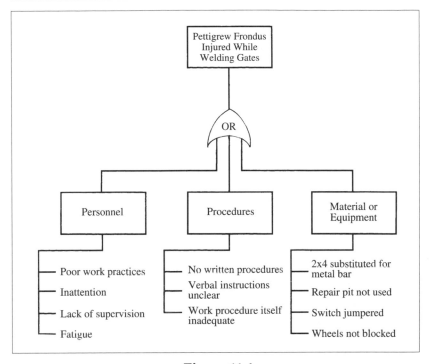

Figure 11.4
Partial Tree Diagram—Accident

factors we just added. For our purposes in describing the process, we will stop at this level and continue with the next steps in root cause tree analysis.

Validating the Tree
After the initial tree diagram has been constructed, the next step is to validate it. Others with knowledge of the situation may be used to help review the events portrayed in the tree for accuracy and completeness.

Using the tree, follow each of the paths through the tree for their "fit" with the accident facts. Do the listed factors suggest the likely occurrence of the event or problem, or one similar to it? Is each factor or subfactor suggested by the facts or otherwise plausible?

One way to check fit is to change the sign and then study the results. For example, in examining Figure 11.4, one factor listed under "personnel" is Pettigrew's fatigue, inferred by successive 14-hour shifts. When examining this factor, consider the reverse: that Pettigrew was fully alert. Had he been so, the quick closure of the doors would still likely have caused the accident. Fatigue therefore becomes less suspect as a direct, singular causal factor unless it influenced other actions; this suggests fatigue might be worthwhile considering as a condition rather than as a causal factor.

Another factor was the use of a 2 x 4 to hold the gates open. While not in accordance with verbal instructions and practice, a welded bar may not be particularly adequate either. After all, welds, particularly tack welds, can also fail. In fact, the story suggests they were usually removed by the simple expedient of striking them with a sledgehammer. This does not suggest either a strong weld or adequate safeguard.

If one were to continue this distillation or decomposition of the initial tree diagram, then the only factor left under personnel would be "poor work practices." Since the factor appears under "personnel," this would refer to Pettigrew's actions, not the procedure itself, which is covered under "procedures." This distinction is important.

What Pettigrew did was unsafe and certainly could be considered poor work practice. In analyzing this factor, we arrive at the conclusion that, although Pettigrew made matters worse, the procedure itself is flawed and inherently unsafe. This is one of those peculiar instances in which "failure to follow procedures" might not be a bad idea. The work procedure itself was inadequate, since doing the work in the prescribed fashion was potentially a dangerous undertaking.

This process of testing and retesting the tree diagram, necessary to the validation process, often results in a number of issues which, while not directly bearing on the particular situation, will warrant future examination. This identification of less than adequate conditions is a valuable by-product, not only of tree diagrams, but also of other root cause analysis techniques. Often the analyst will discover potential situations that are likely to cause future problems and therefore represent opportunities for improvement.

Properly done, the process of validation prunes the tree. Factors that are not part of the problem at hand are eliminated and the diagram thereby greatly simplified; however, it should be pointed out that the validation process also can introduce new elements to the finished diagram.

Modifying the Tree

Any required modifications to the tree diagram should be made and the revised diagram retested. Changes may be based on the verification process described above, new or revised information, or different scenarios suggested during this review process. Avoid the understandable desire to get on with the analysis until you are sure the tree is as complete and accurate as possible. After all, this diagram will be the basis of determinations made in succeeding stages.

Postulating Possible Scenarios

If the tree has been properly validated, then examination of the various paths should allow a number of possible problem scenarios to be postulated. In the introductory story there were several elements to consider as well as a number of possible reasons that the event might have occurred. Remember the logic implied by the gates. Since "OR" gates usually are

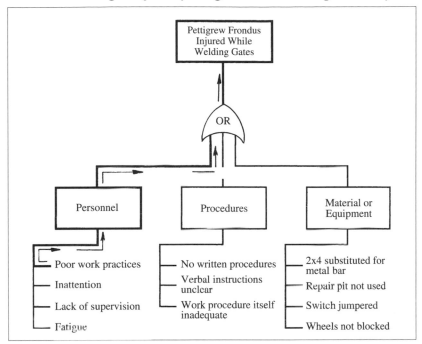

Figure 11.5
Partial Tree Diagram
Highlighting Poor Work Practice Scenario

used in a root cause tree, this implies that the accident or problem could have occurred because of any one, several, or all of the factors listed.

There are a number of ways to perform this step. One method is to use color coding, identifying different paths and combinations on the tree by simply coloring in the blocks and tracing the path. Another, similar technique would be to trace each path using different type lines (dotted, dashed, etc.) or by highlighting each possible path. In Figure 11.5, we show one path through the tree, that of the single factor previously discussed, "poor work practices."

Another version could show "poor work practice" *and* "inattention." In fact, there are as many versions as there are combinations of the various factors taken singly, several or all at a time.

Another technique is to construct a form of truth table, which can be used to list the various paths and their combinations. At this point, it is helpful to begin to assign the predominant cause associated with each of these scenarios.

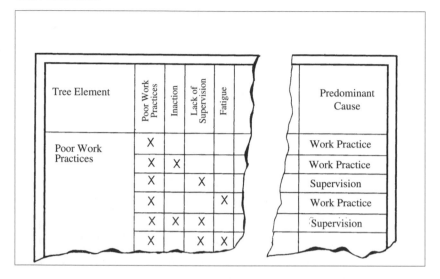

Tree Element	Poor Work Practices	Inaction	Lack of Supervision	Fatigue	Predominant Cause
Poor Work Practices	X				Work Practice
	X	X			Work Practice
	X		X		Supervision
	X			X	Work Practice
	X	X	X		Supervision
	X		X	X	Supervision

Figure 11.6
Partial Truth Table

For example, Figure 11.6 shows a truth table constructed using the tree provided for the introductory story. Although not shown in Figure 11.6 for the obvious reason of available space, all possible scenarios suggested by the facts of the situation should be included.

The reader will now begin to appreciate the value of the previous validation step. The more the tree has been pruned or simplified, the easier this part of the process.

Selecting the Best Scenario

After the above step has been completed, the next step is to select that scenario that best fits the facts of the particular event or problem. The reader, again for purposes of time and space, is now to assume that all possible scenarios have been provided either in a series of coded tree diagrams or in a completed truth table. Several of these scenarios may have been selected as finalists. The selection should include those scenarios most likely to have resulted in the problem in terms of probability and/or the known facts of the particular situation. Many of the possible combinations will have been eliminated because they were not sufficient or capable of causing the particular problem.

Quite often it will be noticed that one or more common "threads" or factors in the scenarios are selected as finalists. As with the mathematical technique, this can be factored out; chances are this was the root cause. The introductory story was constructed around a basically unsafe work procedure. If the analysis was properly performed, this factor would be present in those scenarios selected as likely. Procedures, whether written or not, are part of the overall work planning process, which is ultimately the responsibility of management.

Root Cause Determination

The last step in the process is to determine the root cause of the event or problem based on the inadequacies (causes) identified when listing the possible scenarios. This step is easier if the suggestion of assigning causes to each scenario when initially listing them was followed. In our case, we have already provided the answer. The root cause in the introductory story was less than adequate planning (management methods). The process was inherently unsafe.

Recommendations

Corrective and preventive action recommendations should be based on the event and root cause determination. In the example, the root cause was poor management planning. Unfortunately, management's emphasis on production without due consideration to safety precipitated the accident. Unless changes in work practices, which include adequate safety provisions, are provided as part of the final recommendations, then another accident is likely to occur.

Unfortunately, in real life, the worker often is blamed for not following procedures or inattention to details. If not the worker, then direct supervision is next considered to be at fault. This usually occurs because the fix appears easier, even if ineffective. Since the root cause has been ignored, it should be no surprise that the problem resurfaces.

Process of Prospective Tree Analysis

Tree diagrams can also be used in a positive or proactive manner. For example, the National Aeronautics and Space Administration (NASA) uses tree diagrams to prevent design oversights. Instead of the question, "How did this happen?" the tree is constructed to examine the premise "How can we achieve this goal, wanted event or condition, or desired outcome?" The result becomes a road map that can be used for goal attainment.

The overall process is similar to that used to construct reactive or fault trees, except that the process is now positive. The top event becomes the desired condition or goal. The second level of the tree lists those major elements or factors deemed necessary to attain the goal or desired condition. Branching is done in similar fashion by providing more detailed information or events under each of the major factors or categories. Resulting scenarios (paths through the tree) are then examined for logic, cost, risk, and benefit. The AND logic symbol is used more often on a positive tree, since *all* the listed elements usually are necessary for eventual success. In planning for an operations or activity change or improvement, the categories or factors previously used in root cause analysis are helpful: personnel, equipment or material, and procedures.

To illustrate the concept of a positive tree, consider the simple example of planting a new lawn. Using the major factors or categories of

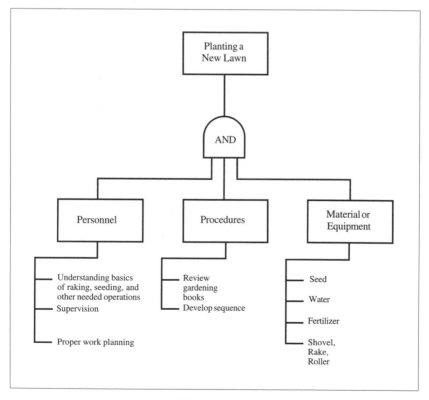

Figure 11.7
Positive Tree

personnel, procedures and material, or equipment, the prospective tree diagram shown in Figure 11.7 was constructed.

Under each of the categories, further definition (similar to the root cause tree) has been provided. The positive tree branches out in the same fashion as before *except* now we are considering all the things necessary for success, rather than evaluating the cause of failure.

Summary

Tree diagrams are relatively easy to construct and to understand; they are extremely visual, depicting problem elements or factors as well as their relationship. Trees can be used to analyze an unwanted event or problem or alternately, to clearly show what must be done to attain specific goals. They are useful in examining paths critical to the success or failure of the event.

One disadvantage of tree diagrams is that they may not always clearly identify the specific cause of events or problems, but only indicate general areas of concern. When this condition occurs, the analyst may have to perform a change or barrier analysis "off to the side" to determine exactly what has happened.

Tree analysis methodology can be used in a variety of situations. Tree diagrams are especially effective in analyzing complex events or situations and therefore can be used to plan or analyze systems, organizations, large or small projects, or plant operations.

Tree diagrams also are useful in analyzing system or equipment failures. Considerable work has already been done in this particular area. Some readers may be familiar with Failure Mode and Effects Analysis (FMEA) as well as the probabilistic trees used in risk analysis.

Key Ideas

- Tree diagrams provide a highly visual display which aids in analyzing the event or problem (in a reactive mode) or in planning goal attainment (in the prospective mode). The display also helps to identify any critical paths to success or failure, as the case may be.
- Tree diagrams are particularly useful in analyzing complex situations since, properly constructed, they include all pertinent factors or elements as well as describing relationships.
- Tree diagrams can easily be combined with or augmented by other root cause analysis techniques.

12

OTHER STRUCTURED ROOT CAUSE ANALYSIS TECHNIQUES

"For want of a method, the results were never gained.
And for want of finding the cause, the problems remained."

—Fractured quotation by the authors (1991)

Introduction

Four basic types of root cause analysis techniques have been presented: change analysis, barrier analysis, events and causal factors, and tree diagrams. Previously, it was pointed out that there are many other structured or formal root cause analysis methods available, although many of these are basically variations, combinations, or extensions of the fundamental types discussed thus far.

This chapter will discuss a few more commonly used formal root cause analysis techniques. The purpose is to informally introduce readers to these methods while instilling the idea that there probably is a root cause analysis technique that will meet your organization's needs (or at least one that can be readily adapted or modified to do so). There is no intention of trying to provide a complete listing of all currently used formal root cause analysis techniques.

Throughout these chapters, it has been continually pointed out that these analysis techniques should be viewed as tools to be used in constructing a truly effective TQM program. A saw is a basic tool, but there are many types of saws: rip, crosscut, hacksaw, jigsaw, etc. Given the more basic mission of cutting material, there could be other tools employed (e.g., scissors, chisels, axes, knives) depending upon the particular situation.

The same concept applies to our analysis tools. A variety of tools are available to do the job. Before becoming enamored of the tools themselves, remember the purpose for which they are being used: to effectively identify problems and through the subsequent process of appropriate corrective and preventive action(s), eliminate their recurrence. The technique's elegance is not nearly as important as the results. A good carpenter does not blame his tools when the desired results are not achieved any more than Michelangelo waited for power or fancier cutting tools to produce his sculptures.

This leads to a twist to the famous philosophical question: Do the means justify the end or does the end justify the means? In our case, this becomes: Does the (root cause) method justify the results or do the results justify the method? If the reader has not realized that the most important aspect of root cause analysis is the *result(s),* the identification of the real reason for problems, the text has failed in communicating this simple message. For those individuals who missed it, let's state it one more time: *The basic purpose of root cause analysis is finding the real reasons problems occur.* The best use of the technique(s) is in preventing problems.

Participants in some of the seminars the authors have conducted will tend to blur or otherwise combine these basic methods, finding the hybrid technique more attuned to the personal way they view and solve problems. Barring introduction of technical or logic faults, there is nothing wrong with this. Once again, the focus should be on the results.

Introductory Story
Without breaking stride with the discussion of tools, consider the following scenario. A radial arm saw is a mechanical marvel. With more flexibility in certain situations than a table saw, it is capable of a wide variety of cutting tasks in the home workshop. Similar to a table saw or portable handheld saw, however, it can be extremely dangerous if operated improperly.

To prevent accidental operation, the power switch on the saw requires that a key be inserted first. For those unfamiliar with the tool, this key is comparable to the plastic cover plugs inserted into electrical outlets to prevent children from poking things into them. It does not look like a key in the usual sense.

The radial arm saw's key is a clever device which works well. Without the key's insertion into the switch, the saw will not run. Due to its small size, it also is easy to lose or misplace. Leaving the key in the switch, although convenient, defeats its purpose. Placing the key conveniently near the saw may negate its safety purpose as well, since it is easy for a child to observe and duplicate the action of inserting the device and operating the saw. Not much training is needed.

Another ploy might be to store it in a safe place. For most individuals, this usually is the equivalent of losing it.

Defense in depth might be obtained by combining the above action with a stern lecture on the danger of (in fact, all) power tools. The macabre set might even couple this lecture with the deliberate cutting of a finger-sized piece of dowel to illustrate the danger. (Those readers with children will quickly realize how lasting this lesson may be. Long-term memory (defined as perhaps over one day) only seems to come with maturity, then, unfortunately, lasts only a short while before it begins to fade again with old age.)

Some readers may suggest that signs both on and around the saw might help. Although the list of chores posted on the refrigerator door might be ignored, surely this sign would somehow be different. The list of possible barriers or safeguards is infinite. The point is that the parents (management) have the potential for a serious incident (accident) for which certain actions (programs, practices) need to be considered and the attendant risks associated with their choice evaluated.

This story will be used to illustrate some of the other structured root cause analysis techniques covered in this chapter, including MORT and cause and effect diagrams.

Management Oversight and Risk Tree Analysis (MORT)

Management Oversight and Risk Tree (MORT) analysis was developed in 1974 under contract to the Energy Research and Development Agency, a predecessor to the current Department of Energy, by EG&G, Idaho.

MORT was developed for and is primarily used in the investigation of accidents or incidents. MORT has a deliberate safety focus. As the name implies, MORT is a tree diagram, albeit an elaborate one. As in all tree diagrams, the top event is the accident or incident under investigation.

As the name also suggests, the next (second) level of the tree includes both management oversight and assumed risk. The basic premise of MORT is that any accident is due either to management oversight(s) or omissions or an (improperly) assumed risk.

The top of the MORT tree is shown in Figure 12.1. The reader should note the logic gates used here, as well as elsewhere in the MORT tree. In Figure 12.1, we see the injury, damage, other costs, lost performance, degraded program, or public impact (top event) being attributable to oversights and omissions OR assumed (accepted) risks.

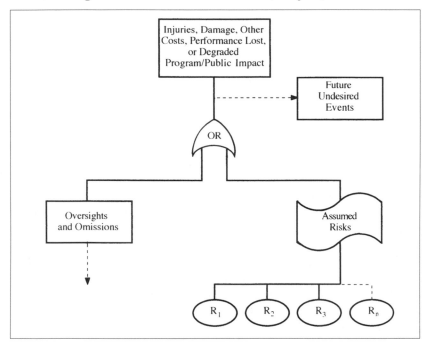

Figure 12.1
Top of MORT-Based Root Cause Tree

Under assumed risks, the tree continues with an OR gate in which any number of assumed risks may be listed, depending on the specific situation. Accepted (assumed) risk is defined as:

Specific, identified, analyzed, quantified to the maximum practicable degree and accepted by the right level of management, after proper evaluation.

Nothing could be clearer. Read the words carefully: management *knew* the odds and *accepted* them. If an event or problem occurs that you knew might happen, but you decided to do nothing based on your assessment of the odds: tough luck, but you just lost your bet. Pay at the door.

Remember our previous discussions on the topic of risk. An organization (through its management) cannot reasonably or practically protect against all contingencies; some risk must be assumed. The key word here is "acceptable."

Following the other main branch, oversights, and omissions, the tree breaks then down into two other subcategories: specific control factors and management system factors. The reader should note in this case that an AND gate is used. The AND logic gate dictates that both must be present; so for each path through the tree on the less-than-adequate specific control factors side, a corresponding path *must* exist for management system factors deemed less than adequate.

Under management system factors less than adequate, the tree branches farther, now again using an OR gate into three elements: policy less-than-adequate or missing (this considered an end event), implementation less-than-adequate and risk assessment less than adequate. (See Figure 12.2.)

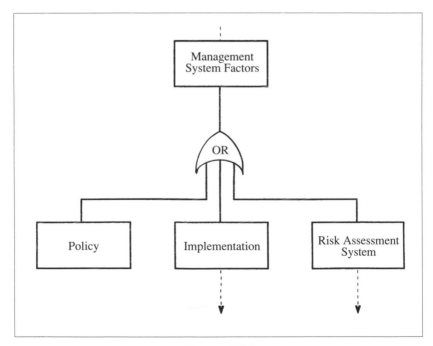

Figure 12.2
MORT Management System Factors

Under specific control factors, the MORT tree breaks down into the following elements: barriers and controls related to the accident or incident, and amelioration using an OR gate. This is shown in Figure 12.3.

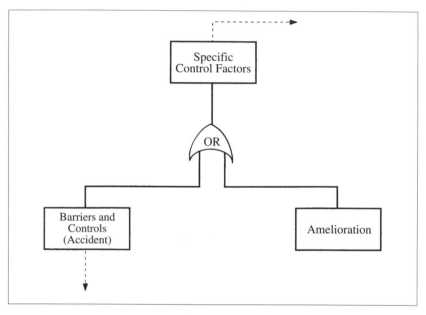

Figure 12.3
MORT Specific Control Factors

Amelioration refers to those responses or actions, whether deliberate or not, that served to limit the consequences of what has occurred and to reduce the sensitivity of those consequences whenever possible. The interesting part of the concept is the examination of these factors to prevent a second accident or further damage. For example, was the emergency response action prompt and adequate? Obviously, this post-event analysis is worthwhile and may eventually result in program or operations changes.

The use of the MORT root cause analysis technique is well documented and prescribed. Each of the elements on the MORT tree has code numbers assigned next to the block. These numbers refer to items contained in an accompanying user's manual which supplies a number of specific questions related to the particular topic (block). There also is reference to the MORT-based root sequence number on an accompanying worksheet. By observing these numbers, asking the suggested questions, following the logic of the tree and completing the accompanying worksheet, the investigator eventually is led to the accident's root cause.

It should be pointed out that the above discussion revolves around what is called the short-form version of MORT. There is a larger, even more detailed, version. The MORT technique virtually ensures that all aspects of the incident or accident are explored.

The current training period for the full-blown MORT (MORT/AI) technique is two weeks. Completion of this training is *required* under present Department of Energy rules for certified accident investigators who continue as sponsors of the MORT analysis technique. The authors' evaluation of MORT (either long- or short-form version) is that it is an entirely satisfactory technique for its intended purpose; however, even the short version may be more elaborate than is necessary for most problems.

The introductory story, while fairly simple, is sufficient to explain some of the concepts of management oversight and risk tree analysis. Since MORT is primarily intended to investigate accidents and events, the authors, mortified at the prospect of postulating an accident involving the saw and children, will merely show how some of the story elements fit the tree. We will discuss them as a non-event.

The top event in our example would therefore be prevention of the accident. Branching down, we would need to define the scenario further to identify the assumed risks. Let us assume we hide the key in a high enough place to prevent children from easily accessing it. Of course, the risk is that they do find it. We can assess this risk rather easily, in terms of the ages of the children (which must be revised later, of course), the general supervision provided, access to the workshop allowed, etc. Note that our thinking is beginning to sound like barrier analysis, which, incidentally, is included as part of the overall MORT process. We could put into place additional barriers, such as locking the workshop or installing a padlocked power switch. Any or all of these additional preventive actions would influence the assessed overall risk, lowering it until it reaches an acceptable value. Readers should also note that, as these additional preventive actions are considered, entries on the other side of the tree will be affected (remember the OR logic) under barriers and controls.

Using the original premise of simply hiding the key, this action would be listed under barriers and controls. If one decides to couple this with a stern lecture (hopefully repeated from time to time, based on the volatility of training in general and short-term memories in particular), this can also be shown as an additional control or barrier. Remember that the assumed risk must factor in this additional element. The elements of the story thus far can be depicted as shown in Figure 12.4 in a MORT tree.

For those readers interested in learning more about this technique, there is considerable literature and training available. There are many

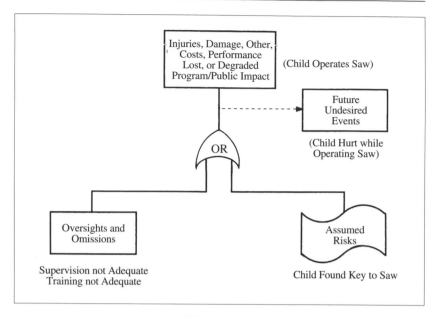

Figure 12.4
Partial MORT—Introductory Story

MORT-related documents in the Suggested Reading list at the end of this book.

Human Performance Evaluation System

Since many of the problems in the nuclear power industry are traceable to human performance, the Institute for Nuclear Power Operations (an industry organization of plant owners and others) sponsors a root cause technique called Human Performance Evaluation. Readers in the service industries may find this technique particularly appropriate.

Human performance evaluation defines three basic types of situations: consequential, nonconsequential, and potential problems. Each of these basic types of situations involves actual or potential inappropriate actions in terms of human performance. Inappropriate action is behavior that turns normal performance into an abnormal situation.

A (hopefully) now-familiar technique is utilized within Human Performance Evaluation (HPE): events and causal factors analysis. The basic steps are as follows:

■ Event reconstruction and analysis
■ Behavioral analysis

- Causal factor analysis
- Situational analysis
- Executive summary

Worksheets are provided to aid the analyst in the process. HPES, as it is usually referred to, is an extremely useful technique for particular situations. It brings into play interesting concepts related to human behavior and performance, task accomplishment evaluations similar to the old industrial engineering studies, man–machine interface (also known as ergonomics), and others.

Cause and Effect
(Fishbone) Diagram

It was almost predictable that the "fishbone" diagram introduced by Dr. Ishikawa some years ago would be adapted for root cause analysis. It is a highly visual technique which aids the process of defining the elements of a problem or event and determining how it probably occurred. Using the logic and the potential contributory elements defined previously (personnel, equipment or material, and procedures), the authors have constructed a basic fishbone diagram (see Figure 12.5).

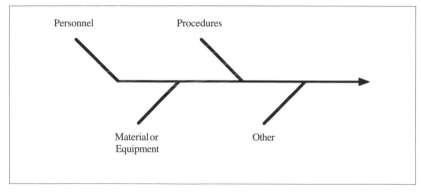

Figure 12.5
Basic Cause and Effect Diagram

Each of the spines could be broken down further. For example, the "procedures" element can be shown as being comprised of the following:

- Procedures available
- Procedures up-to-date
- Procedures accurate and reviewed
- Procedures understandable and clear

This same breakdown was provided earlier in Chapter 11. The further definition of the procedures element of the fishbone diagram is shown in Figure 12.6. Similarly, the other basic elements (personnel and material or equipment) can also be broken into specific factors.

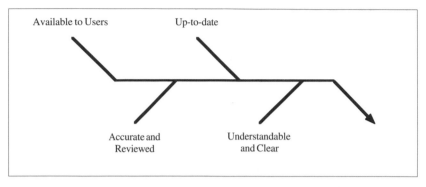

Figure 12.6
Cause and Effect Diagram—Procedures Element

To illustrate the use of a cause and effect diagram, once again refer to the introductory story of the radial arm saw. Although a simple example, some of the elements are present, including:

■ Personnel–communications, supervision, training
■ Equipment–design, operation, interlocks
■ Procedures–rules of operation

These elements may be shown in a cause-and-effect diagram (see Figure 12.7) to illustrate the concept.

Cause-and-effect diagrams should not be confused with events and causal factors analysis. Remember that events and causal factors analysis

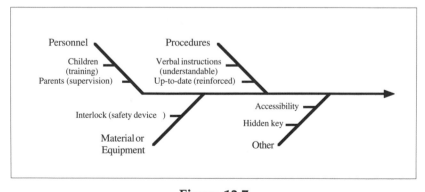

Figure 12.7
Cause and Effect Diagram—Introductory Story

had an event line with a time/sequence dimension with conditions and causal factors linked to these events. The fishbone diagram is subject-oriented. There probably is a closer similarity of cause-and-effect diagrams to tree diagrams. Cause-and-effect diagrams may be visualized as a tree diagram lying on its side. This may be helpful to some readers in understanding the methodology employed. Similar to the tree diagram, a clear, unbroken line or path must exist between the real causal factor and the final event. A condition or element might be noted as less than adequate (and for this reason alone ultimately require correction), but unless there is a trace to the final event or problem, this factor was not the culprit (at least not this time).

For those who might wish to adopt the cause-and-effect technique, there are no rules (to the authors' knowledge) on "mixing and matching" methods. The fishbone technique is straightforward and extremely useful for certain kinds of problem analysis. More octane might be added by including the logic gating techniques from tree diagrams or the condition(s) notations from events and causal factors analysis. These embellishments might help the application of cause-and-effect diagrams in more complex situations.

As with the other root cause analysis methods covered herein, the fishbone also is suited for use in a prospective mode. It can be constructed in a positive sense, becoming a road map for goal attainment. Comparable to tree diagrams and event and causal factors diagrams, the fishbone enjoys the particular advantage of a highly visual, easy-to-understand and reader-friendly format.

Other Techniques

It should be recognized that there are many other structured root cause analysis methods available. One of the initial choices in preparing this book was whether to provide trivial coverage of the many or complete coverage of a vital few. The decision was easy. If the reader becomes familiar with the four basic techniques included in this text, he/she should be able to quickly understand how most of the other methods work. In fact, if the authors were to list *all* of the techniques currently available, the odds are that by the time we went to press or certainly shortly thereafter, this list would be obsolete.

Currently there is much interest in the overall subject of root cause analysis, the finding of the real reason problems occur and by this identification process, finding ways to eliminate them. As mentioned earlier, the elegance or choice of technique is far less important than the determination to find and solve organizational problems at their most basic level.

Summary

The purpose of this chapter was to acquaint readers with some other commonly used root cause analysis techniques. Those interested in pursuing any of the methods mentioned in this chapter will find the necessary references in the Suggested Reading List.

One of the hidden agendas in writing this book was to create a certain amount of anxiety in the readers. One cause for anxiety might be that we are not doing all the right things to find and fix problems in our organizations. Another cause is that, having found these problems, we tend to either avoid taking the needed action(s) or prefer to prescribe our own favorite remedies, whether or not they work. The final cause for anxiety is that we fail to see obvious opportunities for improvement and (since we cannot see them), feel no urgency to act on them. The authors are banking on the psychologists being correct. If an anxiety exists, it will create a tension, which in turn will produce action to relieve that tension.

The one concept that best summarizes this chapter is that there are *many* root cause analysis techniques available which can either (1) be used directly or (2) be easily adapted for your organization's needs. Don't have the impression that all those fancy root cause analysis techniques are really impressive, but they obviously won't work in your particular and unique situation. Find one that does; there are certainly enough from which to choose. The Suggested Reading list includes a number of systems that represent modifications of some of the basic techniques discussed in this book to fit a particular organization's needs. The reader who is interested in certain applications of these root cause methods is encouraged to read these articles and books and study what others have done. The intent herein has been to equip you with a fundamental set of tools and counsel you in choosing wisely.

13

SUMMARY

"This journey is never finished."

—The authors, 1991

Introduction

Most readers probably will agree that there has been a considerable amount of material presented in this book. The intention was to present an overview of root cause analysis concepts and some of the techniques employed. The text started by describing root cause analysis techniques as a vital element of a TQM program, then proceeded to define the concepts of accurately identifying root causes and the value of fixing problems at that basic level. There was discussion of the idea of lining up problems, causes, and proposed solutions to ensure that the problem did not recur.

A number of basic root cause methods were discussed. The intention in doing so was, of course, to demonstrate the variety of techniques that are available, rather than endorse one method over the other. In fact, throughout the book, emphasis has been placed on the graded approach, choosing the method of analysis which fits the severity or consequences of the particular problem at hand. The attempt was made to present these root cause methods evenly, discussing both their strengths and weaknesses as well as their usual applications. It has also been suggested that these techniques, barring the introduction of logic faults, can be adapted or modified to be more useful.

Throughout the chapters, the prospective use of these techniques has been stressed. This is believed to be the *best* application of these techniques, and the authors wholeheartedly endorse their use in this mode. The rationale here is that, if your organization is utilizing these methods to identify the most obvious candidates for improvement, it is reasonable to assume that you have reached the third plateau discussed below. You have successfully solved your current problems and eliminated current obstacles to improvement. In short, you have arrived.

The Destination
Having arrived, the obvious question might be: Where are we? Earlier in the book, there was allusion to the fact that there are different levels at which organizations might presently be operating. The first level is the finding and correcting of problems, with many being washed downstream. Unfortunately, those individuals washed downstream are internal and external clients and customers. An organization obviously cannot hope to maintain its position with this handicap.

The second level is the organization finding and fixing problems in such a manner that they do not recur. Fewer problems end up with the clients and customers. Sooner or later, the organization will catch up with these surfaced problems and then should expect to be able to at least maintain its present position with minimal effort.

The third level is that in which the organization seeks to *prevent* problems or faults. They do not allow them to occur. This is the prospective mode. Problems simply are not introduced into the system, therefore they do not occur nor do they need to be fixed. Things are done right the first time.

This then is the destination at which organizations should plan to arrive. Using efforts to improve current operations is the most basic idea behind total quality management.

Total Quality Management

Considering what has occurred, whoever first coined this term might wish to reconsider the phrasing. Total Quality Management is somewhat a misnomer, because in the attempts to put TQM into practice, organizations have misinterpreted it as a quality function. This is only partially true. Most accurately, it is an overall management function.

Many companies, desiring to jump onto the TQM bandwagon, have assigned the development and implementation of a TQM program to the quality manager. After all, it says quality, doesn't it? In reality, the chief operating officer should be the sponsor, developer, and implementer. Not every organization has realized that quality was *never* the sole responsibility of the quality manager; only its control and assurance.

Quality problems are the problems of the operations and activities managers, the financial and marketing managers, in short, *all* managers. It also is the responsibility of the workers and operators. Problems affect the entire organization. The quality manager's role is reporting and helping to fix problems. In a well-run organization, the quality manager's job should be the easiest. Everyone else is doing what they should.

One other aspect of TQM that is overlooked by virtue of its title is productivity. Everyone *knows* productivity and quality are inextricably linked. Unlike the control of quality, which most often has a negative implication, increased productivity always is viewed positively. What is most often forgotten is that the two go together.

For the readers, then, perhaps the rest of the definition should be *total quality, productivity, improvement and effective management program.* This may not catch on, but it describes what the program is about.

The Malcolm Baldrige National Quality Award

The Malcolm Baldrige National Quality Award, named for the late U.S. Secretary of Commerce, was established by act of Congress in 1987. The goals of this award are to promote quality awareness, recognize quality leadership and achievement, and publicize successful quality strategies. Organizations are graded on the following.

- Leadership in creating and maintaining a quality culture
- The effectiveness of information and analysis in planning quality
- Strategic quality planning
- Effective human resource utilization
- Quality assurance activities
- Quality achievement and improvement
- Customer satisfaction

Readers no doubt will note the similarity of the above items with concepts discussed in this book, as well as the basic premise of an effective TQM program. This correlation should come as no surprise.

Process and Activity Improvement

Throughout the book, we have pointed to effective root cause analysis as a necessary tool for overall process or activity improvement. Root cause analysis will identify the real cause of problems or unwanted events in current operations. These conditions, if corrected, should preclude occurrence of these faults.

The authors would be remiss in their obligations to the readers unless they pointed out that the mere identification of the cause of these problems or unwanted conditions does not somehow automatically assure their correction. As rigor is required during the process of isolating and identifying these causes, similar exactitude is needed to devise effective corrective, preventive, or adaptive actions.

Regarding the use of these results to identify candidates for improvement, how can you improve a process or activity if you do not understand how it operates? How can you reduce inconsistencies if you have no idea of the process' inherent variation?

The point is that the output of root cause analysis must be linked to the other needed elements of TQM, such as effective process project/process management (which includes process capability studies, analysis, and reduction of variance, etc.), fault correction, performance-based assessment, trend analysis, etc. (refer to Figure 1.1). Root cause analysis is only one piece of the puzzle. Although root cause analysis is a vital element of any quality and productivity program, it is most effective when used in conjunction with the others that also are needed.

The Prognosis

Readers who have followed the book thus far may be dismayed at the fact that all that has been provided is still not enough. More work may be ahead. Other complementary systems must be considered and installed for the program to work. The alternative, however, is far less appealing.

If we do not get started, regardless of how far it seems we have to go, we will be left behind. That prospect should be sufficiently chilling to spur action. As with any prognosis, there must be an estimate of the chances of recovery.

There is considerable inertia involved with the implementation of any system, perhaps more so with one that represents a radical departure from the way things have been done previously. There probably will be considerable discomfort. There may even be some genuine pain associated with the development and implementation of root cause analysis systems. On the other hand, however, there exists some fertile ground in which to plant this concept. Most people are tired of fixing the same old problem, tired of constantly trying to catch up, convinced that there are better ways of doing things; in short, people are receptive, at least at the gut level, for meaningful change.

As with the previous discussion of change, change can be considered as having two aspects. The merit of the proposed changes needs little elaboration; it is the means of implementing these changes that is important. Quality circles were largely doomed to failure in those organizations which failed to effectively listen to, consider, and implement the recommended actions. Similarly, root cause analysis will be predictably ineffective in those organizations which cannot accurately identify faults and problems, provide less-than-adequate analyses because of staffing or training, fail to act on proposed solutions or translate the results into more palatable solutions, regardless of their merit. Perhaps, like the recovering alcoholic, these organizations must first be willing to declare openly that they indeed have a problem.

Some Closing Thoughts

The authors truly appreciate the patience of those readers who have stuck with us this far. There has been a lot of "preachifying" in this book along with the different concepts presented. This has occurred because of our belief that all that has been included in these chapters is vitally important.

This book could have been subtitled *Effective Problem Solving*, but this would have been only partially true. It also is about problem avoidance, which seems more appropriate.

This text has been about finding and fixing problems, but there also has been an attempt to apply a reasonable balance to this process, suggesting a graded approach to this effort. It has been pointed out that some problems are not worth fixing at all, but that appropriate adaptive action should be taken (similiar to driving around potholes). It has also been cautioned that certain problems are embedded in the processes and activities themselves and that only modification of the basic operations will ultimately result in their elimination.

We have advocated the concept that, in any organization, finding and fixing problems is everyone's responsibility and we have attempted to convince the reader that it is to everyone's advantage to do so. We have promoted the use of these problem solving methods in a prospective mode, to identify the most obvious candidates for improvement. We believe this use to be the best use of the techniques.

Perhaps some anxieties have been created. One anxiety might be that we are not doing all we could reasonably do to improve our present operations. We have given you some tools to use and then told you that their use is up to you. More questions may have been raised than answers provided.

There is only so much that can (or should) be covered in any one book. Recognizing that an overview has been provided of most of the subjects covered and that further practice will be necessary to sharpen application skills, there is an accompanying workbook which provides step-by-step analyses of more complex problems. The reader who desires to do so is invited to learn by doing.

We have attempted to show the importance of effective root cause analysis as one of the vital elements in any quality and productivity program, such as total quality management. We cautioned that these other elements must be present to build a firm foundation on to construct the program.

In addition to all this information and advice, we have added the final argument: we know it will work because we have *seen* it work. It can work for you too.

SUGGESTED READING

Armor, A. F., J. B. Parkes, and D. E. Leaver. "Root Cause Analysis of Fossil Plant Equipment Failures: The EPRI Program." *IEEE Trans. Power Apparat. Syst.,* June 1981.

ASQC Quality Costs Committee. *Principles of Quality Costs,* John T. Hagan, ed. Milwaukee: ASQC Quality Press, 1986.

Benner, L., Jr. "Accident Investigations: Multilinear Events Sequencing Method," *J. Safety Res.,* June 1975.

Chiu, C. *Root Cause Guidebook,* San Clemente: Failure Prevention, Inc., 1989.

Clausing, D. and B. H. Simpson. "Quality by Design," *Qual. Progr.,* January 1990.

Cornelison, J. D. *MORT Based Root Cause Analysis,* Idaho Falls: System Safety Development Center, May 1989.

Cushing, N., J. Cauble, and C. Perrin. "Partners in Quality," *Communique,* March 1990.

Dew, J. R. "In Search of the Root Cause," *Qual. Progr.,* July 1991.

Dibble, D. "An Open Letter to the PCB Industry," *Energy Update,* March 1991.

Gano, D. L. "Root Cause and How to Find It," *Nucl. News,* August 1987.

Juran, J. M. *Juran on Leadership for Quality—An Executive Handbook,* New York: The Free Press, 1989.

Keltner, W. G. "Effective Root Cause Analysis—A View from a Government Facility," Paper presented at the 16th Ann. Nat'l Energy Divi. Conf.

Kepner, C. H. and B. B. Tregoe. *The New Rational Manager,* Princeton: Kepner-Tregoe, Inc., 1981.

Knox, N. W. and R. W. Eicher. *MORT User's Manual,* SSDC-4. Idaho Falls: EG&G, Idaho, Inc., May 1983.

Ledbetter, W. *The Quality Performance Management System: A Blueprint for Implementation,* Austin: The Construction Industry Institute, February 1989.

Mager, R. F. and P. Pipe. *Analyzing Performance Problems,* Belmont, CA: Fearon Pitman Publishers, 1970.

Nertney, R. J., J. D. Cornelison, and W. A. Trost. *Root Cause Analysis of Performance Indicators,* WP-21. Idaho Falls: System Safety Development Center, April 1989.

Peranich, M. W. "The Operating Reactor Inspection Program and Guidance for Inspection of Root Cause," Paper presented at the 16th Ann. Energy Div. Conf.

Slater, R. H. "Integrated Process Management: A Quality Model," *Qual. Prog.,* May 1991.

Stratton, B. "What Makes It Take? What Makes It Break?" *Qual. Progr.,* April 1990.

Wilson, P. F. and L. D. Dell. *Introduction to Root Cause Analysis,* Richland: Quality Resource and Training Center, May 1991.

—— *Creating a Quality Culture: Root Cause Analysis,* Richland: Quality Resource and Training Center, March 1990.

Weed, J. F. "The Elusive Root Cause of a Problem," *Energy Update,* December 1989.
—— *Utility-Oriented Approach for Root Cause Analysis of Power Plant Equipment Problems,* Palo Alto: Electric Power Research Institute, 1981.
—— *Root Cause Analysis* INPO 90-004. Atlanta: Institute for Nuclear Power Operations, January 1990.

INDEX